D1715187

Adult Development

Adult Development

Cognitive Aspects of Thriving Close Relationships

JAN D. SINNOTT

Oxford University Press is a department of the University of
Oxford. It furthers the University's objective of excellence in research,
scholarship, and education by publishing worldwide.

Oxford   New York
Auckland   Cape Town   Dar es Salaam   Hong Kong   Karachi
Kuala Lumpur   Madrid   Melbourne   Mexico City   Nairobi
New Delhi   Shanghai   Taipei   Toronto

With offices in
Argentina   Austria   Brazil   Chile   Czech Republic   France   Greece
Guatemala   Hungary   Italy   Japan   Poland   Portugal   Singapore
South Korea   Switzerland   Thailand   Turkey   Ukraine   Vietnam

Oxford is a registered trademark of Oxford University Press
in the UK and certain other countries.

Published in the United States of America by
Oxford University Press
198 Madison Avenue, New York, NY 10016

© Oxford University Press 2014

All rights reserved. No part of this publication may be reproduced, stored in
a retrieval system, or transmitted, in any form or by any means, without the prior
permission in writing of Oxford University Press, or as expressly permitted by law,
by license, or under terms agreed with the appropriate reproduction rights organization.
Inquiries concerning reproduction outside the scope of the above should be sent to the
Rights Department, Oxford University Press, at the address above.

You must not circulate this work in any other form
and you must impose this same condition on any acquirer.

Library of Congress Cataloging-in-Publication Data
Sinnott, Jan D.
Adult development : cognitive aspects of thriving close relationships / Jan D. Sinnott.
   pages cm
Includes bibliographical references and index.
ISBN 978–0–19–989281–5 (hardback)
1. Interpersonal relations.   2. Adulthood—Psychological aspects.   I. Title.
HM1106.S563 2014
302—dc23   2014012121

9 8 7 6 5 4 3 2 1
Printed in the United States of America
on acid-free paper

Contents

Preface

I'm a psychologist. People have two common reactions to that fact when they meet me and find out my profession. One reaction is something like fear and silence, because we all worry at least a little that we're pathological in some way and don't want others to see our weaknesses. But the other reaction always, in some way, demonstrates a curiosity about relationships. "What can you tell me about (name problem here) that I always have with my mother/father/partner/family member/friend?" Of course I can't say very much about their problematic relationship since I usually don't know the person involved in it. But this intense interest in close relationships is evident all around me, all around us, often in our own thoughts and feelings as we go through the day. We yearn for close relationships. We want to understand them, get some control over them, if for no other reason than to manage the strong feelings that come with them. And we *need* close relationships. After all, we are a social species.

I'm a psychologist, and psychology does have a lot to tell us about our close relationships but in my opinion, not enough. We seem to be short-changing a part of the Big Picture. Something seems incomplete to me as I read studies about relationships. In this topic I know quite a lot about, something important seems to be missing.

I have spent years thinking about thinking, and wisdom, and how the quality of our thinking ability alters our life experience as we develop. I have spent years looking at problem-solving abilities of adults and at the outcomes of those abilities in behavior in all kinds of settings. But in all of that investigation where was our understanding of problem-solving and thinking ability in the relationship setting? That question, as I framed it for myself, relates to the thinking abilities I had been studying. Does it matter if a person is able to think in complex ways in the setting of a close relationship? If so, *how* might it matter? If it doesn't matter, then thinking certainly plays a disappointing and limited role in one of the most important human experiences. No, I don't believe that we are completely rational animals. We now know that even economic decisions are moved by feelings more than by reason. Maybe relationships are like that too, based mostly on feelings and less on reason. If so, there would not be much information on the role of thinking ability in satisfying relationships. Yet reason would still be at least a part of the relationship story.

Suddenly it hit me. As cognitive psychologists, we have been working hard looking at reasoning and at what is termed the solution of "well-structured" problems. These are problems that have clear goals and clear strategies leading to a single logical solution. But close relationships present *"ill*-structured problems," those dependent on what researchers call "fuzzy set logic." These types of problems often do not have clear goals or solutions or use typical straightforward, scientific logic.

So we psychologists have not yet examined the effect of thinking and problem-solving ability on close relationships. We have been busy elsewhere in the world of well-structured problems.

Of course, understanding the way intimate dyads solve problems that occur in their relationships is critically important to those relationships continuing happily for a long period of time. Many types of family and couple therapy are, bottom line, ways of improving the activity of problem-solving among intimates. Ideally, in therapy we learn to expand the problem space and see the situation from a larger reasoning perspective. This book is partly about *how*, cognitively, this might come about.

At this point you may be thinking about your close relationships and immediately feeling the *feelings* that come with the thought of those relationships. Much of the current work on close relationships is about those feelings—how they are established, maintained, or healed if something goes wrong. For example, in the literature there is consideration of a person's attachment history and its effect on current adult relationships. That feeling component is certainly important, crucial even, to close relationship quality.

But we now know that there are additional things that are important to relationship quality. Credit that new awareness to the emerging global village we all now experience to some degree. When you wander from village to village you notice that other people do things differently. It took a long time, but eventually we psychologists noticed that cultural, historical, and social forces influence relationship quality. Psychology has always been guilty of a certain amount of navel gazing, looking at the person alone as the source of behavior. Psychology came of age in Western culture during the Enlightenment period of history, so the focus on the isolated *individual* became strong. That historical fact in itself is an example of the reality that culture, social expectations, and historical influences are constantly surrounding us like the air we breathe. We did not notice them all around us at first, or consider their effects on us, on our psychology. Cultures and historical periods set up rules and expectations for the conduct of behavior, including behavior related to close relationships. Once we noticed that "air" around us we could begin to study the big picture, the larger stage on which our close relationships play out during our lifetimes. The study of close relationships could be about more than feelings and emotion. We now are becoming aware that this is the first historical period when feelings and emotion can be combined with cognition when considering important elements in close relationships.

Once we, as psychologists, opened our consideration of elements in close relationships to consideration of cultural and historical forces, we set up a situation demanding that we ask more questions about complex causes of behavior related to relationships. Personally, I was motivated to ask the question I am now asking in this book. Looking at one more potentially important factor, I started asking, "What is the importance of the *quality of thinking and of problem-solving ability* for experience and behavior and satisfaction in close relationships?" And I began to see that complex thinking and problem-solving abilities were crucial to behavior and satisfaction in relationships, as well as in other aspects of life.

I began to apply my own theory of complex postformal thought to address the causes of satisfaction or dissatisfaction in close relationships. My theory was built to go beyond Piaget's theory, since mature adult thinkers and problem-solvers don't seem to stay within Piaget's scientific formal logic but go beyond it. What do they do? How do they think if they are wise? There seemed to be "new" logics out there used by wise individuals, by physicists, by mystics, by chaos theory, by theories of self-regulating systems. How did thinking and problem-solving look in these systems, with these thinkers? A self-referential reasoning was used, one that admitted the fact that our truths are partially constructed by us. This cognition seemed to be used in lots of domains of life, so why not within the ever-changing adventure of intimate relationships?

This book starts with an introduction to the complex topic of complex thinking and problem-solving as it relates to intimate relationships (Chapter 1). When I use the term "intimate relationships" I mean couple and spousal relationships *and* close, emotionally intimate relationships between adult siblings and between adult "good friends." The dynamics of satisfying close relationships may or may not have a sexual component. Similar problem-solving abilities would be needed for long-term satisfaction in any of these intimate relationships. Examples and research in this book may focus on any type of intimate relationships. Most of the literature in this field tends to focus on intimate spouses and partners.

Chapter 2 is a discussion of the nature and development of complex postformal thought, looking at some mechanisms in play in that thought process. These processes are related to close relationships.

Chapter 3 examines the specific cognitive operations that constitute postformal thought. In this chapter we also begin a very important discussion of the advanced scientific thought that underlies my theory of postformal complex thought. What kind of reasoning is used by thinkers in, for example, quantum physics? What complex reasoning is part of theories of self-constructing, self-regulating living systems? It turns out that complex postformal thought comes into play in the thinking of the new sciences, demonstrating how such thought is a valuable thinking tool.

Chapter 4 addresses emotionally experienced connections and close relationships and their relation to complex thought. When emotion and connections with others are added to the mix how do we maintain our ongoing "self"? Can we maintain the self and still have strong *felt* connections with our intimates? Or must we lose the self to find intimacy?

Chapter 5 highlights some very important and sometimes very recent social, cultural, and historical factors, all of which interface with cognitive aspects of intimate relationships. Understanding relationships is difficult under the best of circumstances, so it is not surprising that we turn away from an even bigger picture, that of the social forces within which those human interactions are nested. When we psychologists study the *cognitive* aspects of these relationships, we may be especially tempted to focus on the individual who does that thinking, rather than on variables surrounding that individual thinker. Chapter 5 calls attention to just a few of the recent analyses that might prove useful in our thinking about these broader variables and relationships.

When we reach Chapter 6 we are ready to use our new, sophisticated lens to examine the available research literature on cognition and close relationships. Some of these studies led to the variables included in my own empirical research on relationships, research described later in this book. Analyses of some implications for relationship satisfaction of having (or not having) access to postformal thought are summarized in Chapter 6. There are implications for happiness vs. unhappiness in intimate relationships. What happens when one partner has access to postformal thought and the other one does not? How does the cognitive ability of a partner relate to healing in a distressed relationship?

Some preliminary qualitative and quantitative research on cognition and intimate relationships is described in Chapter 7. We have found that complex thought is related to relationship satisfaction and to processes that couples and other intimate dyads use within their relationships. In this chapter we meet some couples and intimate dyads living in long-term relationships, dyads who agreed to respond to structured interview questions about their relationship processes and satisfaction. We can see from their responses that some of the complex thought elements discussed more abstractly in earlier chapters of the book have real-life expressions in the interactions of real dyads. These responses support earlier research in which happy and less happy dyads were videotaped solving problems together.

Chapter 8 gives a summary of cognitive factors in relationships that *thrive,* factors that go beyond the routine and "just hanging on" levels of interactions. Knowledge of these factors enables us to suggest exercises for individuals or couples who want to grow their interaction skills using postformal complex-thought skills. Increased complexity in thinking about their relationships leads to more adaptive behavior and greater satisfaction for those couples.

Finally, in Chapter 9, we will consider some potential quantitative and qualitative research that is needed if we are to learn more about complex thinking and problem-solving and dyad satisfaction in intimate relationships. Some areas that need further exploration include understanding the ways that complex thought in intimate relationships can be developed. This means creating applications that can be used by dyads to improve their interactions and happiness together and as individuals. What these sorts of applications and tools can give dyads is a new way of seeing their world.

The complex series of factors involved in cognitive aspects of intimate relationships that are satisfying are summarized in Figure 2, in Chapter 5. The caption to Figure 2 gives you a clue to the whole process of creating and understanding cognitive aspects of intimate relationships that are satisfying: "The Circular Evolving Relationship: Cognitive Constructions of Intimate Relationships and Cognitive Constructions of Cultural, Social, and Historical Relationships Co-Construct Each Other Over Time." Figure 2 presents the "Big Picture."

I invite you on this adventure of thinking about a new "big picture" area of exploration: cognitive aspects of intimate relationships that thrive.

Acknowledgments

It is impossible to adequately thank all those who influenced or had a role in these ideas and this book. The conversations and consultations with individuals over my entire life and career have led to what I can offer today in this volume.

I want to thank my whole extended family for the love and experiences they have shared with me, helping me to create theory and research about intimate relationships. I hope the ideas presented here enrich the lives of all my grandchildren as they create intimate relationships in the future. Thanks go to Towson University for its support of my work. Thanks are also due to my friends and colleagues who shared thoughts and emotions with me over the years, helping me grow in so many ways. Special thanks go to my colleague Kate Price, who supported the dream of creating this book and offered so many suggestions for activities for intimates, suggestions offered in a chapter here. Special thanks also to Carol Hoare, who led me to work with Oxford University Press and the excellent staff there. I thank all the reviewers of the book prospectus and of the final manuscript, reviewers willing to contribute suggestions and ideas that made the work better. I appreciate the contributions of students from my Complex Problem Solving Research Lab (in alphabetical order): Travis Geissler, Shelby Hilton, Jen Merson, Ana Nardini, Rachel

Newman, Alyssa Probst, Ryan Schluter, Emily Spanos, and Corie Tippett.

Thank you to the wonderful professional staff at Oxford University Press! Sarah Harrington provided help and feedback regarding the prospectus for this volume and editing of the manuscript. Andrea Zekus was a great help with the finished manuscript, indexing, art, and design. Thank you to Emily Perry, who worked so hard overseeing production and did not get too angry with my missing deadlines.

It is certainly true that "it takes a village" to complete a piece of work. May we always remember that we're all in this together.

Jan Sinnott

Adult Development

Introduction
Complex Thought and Adult Intimate Relationships

T HIS BOOK DESCRIBES SOME UNDERLYING COGNITIVE PROCESSES that interact with emotional and social factors to support satisfying interactions in close relationships. Potentially, relationships can grow stronger and richer when couples can think about their partner and the relationship in more complex ways. This book offers a new way of thinking about relationships, and it may be a rich starting point for research and applications in many settings, for example, in therapy.

Amazingly, there is a lack of information about the ways in which cognition and especially problem-solving abilities might intersect with relational processes in satisfying and less satisfying relationships. Extensive reviews of literature on intimate relationships—couple, friend, familial—have produced surprisingly few resources and findings in this area of study. Here it is not a matter of competing theoretical stances; it is a problem of a virtual lack of theory and research of any sort.

The information in this book explains one way in which complex problem-solving skills can make intimate relationships richer and more satisfying. It develops an extension of my theory and research program on the development, and uses, of complex postformal thought during adulthood and aging. The book rests on 30 years of research in adult cognitive development and on other recent empirical research that I and others have conducted. Cases are presented to illustrate the thinking of persons in close and satisfying relationships. Future research and applications are suggested in the final chapter of the book.

Postformal complex thinking and reasoning seems useful for relating in a satisfying way to those who are close to us, as we shall see later in this book. But we don't always have satisfying relationships with those close to us. Some reasons for this unhappiness can be found by examining emotional life, attachments, maturity, and social situations and expectations. Other reasons for less satisfying interactions with those closest to us may be connected with our ability to *think* about our relationships and our partners. In the case of relationships, more complex types of thought may be useful to allow us to experience satisfying, loving, long-term interactions that are not derailed by the difficulties of life or the differences between us. It may be useful to a relationship to be a good problem-solver.

One way to think about the complexity of thought is found in Piaget's theory, which conceptualizes reasoning thought as an *adaptive, problem-solving* process. In that theory, adults are considered to be capable of scientific, reasoning ("formal thought") views of the world, and of each other.

Three large problems are immediately apparent, however, when we start to think about applying theories of Piagetian scientific formal reasoning thought to relationships. First, adults do not routinely think like scientists, especially when those adults are living day to day in their intimate relationships. Second, studies using Piaget's original problem-solving tasks leave us with the impression that very few adults use scientific formal thought at all and, therefore, that adults generally are mediocre problem-solvers when tested in this way. So how could this thinking ability be helpful for adults developing their intimate relationships? The third problem in applying theories of Piagetian scientific formal reasoning thought to relationships is that people who are trying to have satisfying relationships by being scientific about them (Piaget's most advanced problem-solving type of cognition in his original work) are likely to have an even more difficult time in relationships with that strictly cognitive approach.

One of the new approaches I have used in my research involves the creation and use of problems that tap a type of logical, adaptive problem-solving that is a step more complex than scientific formal-level Piagetian tasks, a reasoning I call *postformal thought*. This complicated reasoning seems to be what adults use in *everyday* problem-solving tasks. Using these materials (originally compared with Piagetian traditional tasks for validity), colleagues and I have demonstrated that many more adults express much more sophisticated reasoning in problem-solving when it is presented in everyday problem settings. In our research, the use of complex postformal thought in those everyday settings was more frequent than we anticipated. Use of even some of the operations of postformal thought seemed to be beneficial to adults in solving everyday relationship problems presented in studies. What the adults with more satisfying relational outcomes were *thinking* as they conceptualized the problems, conceptualized their partners, and conceptualized their relationships seemed to be rather sophisticated reasoning thought that was a level above scientific formal logic. Of course, thought always interacted with emotion, leading to the final outcome of relationship quality. If adults use a different sort of logic, built on Piaget's theory but more complex than Piaget's original theory, some of the problems with applying reasoning thought to close relationships might be solved.

But thinking about this first problem, that adults don't routinely think like scientists, in this new way, we realized that they don't have to think like traditional scientists. Respondents are using a type of thinking that goes beyond scientific thought to a different level of complexity.

Considering the second problem, that very few adults used scientific reasoning in Piagetian studies, when adults expressed their solutions *postformally*, they only appeared to be "failing" at scientific problem-solving, because they were doing something even more complex than scientific problem-solving. They could describe this complex thought, but only when they were asked to do so.

With regard to the third problem, that people have a difficult relational time when they approach relationships using mainly scientific thinking, we need to consider the possibility that intimates in satisfying relationships go *beyond* scientific thought to a higher-level complexity of thought in a relationship situation, coordinating cognitive and emotional approaches.

As I developed my theory of postformal thought, based on the sophisticated thinking and problem-solving of people working with everyday problems like those in relationships, I began to see just how useful this approach is to explain many facets of behavior in the real world.

My complex postformal thought theory *is* complex and different. It is also a simple but elegant idea that can be applied to many types of behavior. My goal as a professional and as a researcher has always been "to go where no one has gone before," since some areas of study are more well researched than others. My initial question was simple: What are adults doing when they appear to be failing Piaget's traditional tasks, but seem to be succeeding in life? For that matter, how can an Einstein or mystics or physicists possibly think like they do and continue to function in everyday life?

Although the "logics" of new physics and mysticism sound very different, at one level they both demand one very special skill, the conscious *co-creation of truth*. They demand that we understand our own role in known reality. The many research applications of my theory (for example, to the quality of intimate adult relationships) are pretty straightforward applications of that underlying ability, to know that we partly co-create truth. This complex cognitive underlying ability can be used without anyone understanding some of the more esoteric models I personally find useful in thinking about complex postformal thought—for example, the theories of general systems theory, the "new" physics of relativity and quantum mechanics, chaos theory, and theories of self-constructing systems.

For most of us, relationships, especially close relationships, are some of the most important things in life. We are a social species. Close relationships reach to the very heart of our happiness. Over a lifetime, we see some intimate relationships become richer and more meaningful to us, while others pale in importance, wither, and die. Ironically, sometimes the more we grasp and fight to keep an important relationship alive, the more we are sure that we know "what's going on" concerning the "reality" of the relationship or the partner, the less the relationship seems to thrive. What is it that helps us learn to relate more deeply, stay open to possible truths of the relationship, and grow past the differences and problems that might divide us?

Adult development and aging are usually examined from the point of view of loss. This book, by contrast, discusses *positive* adult development in the context of close relationships. It extends my theory by focusing on the ways complex thought (postformal complex thought) is important in creating and sustaining the close ongoing relationships between intimate partners, between parents and children, between siblings, and between close friends. This is not a claim that cognition is the *only* important thing in a close relationship, which is patently false. Rather, this book is written from the perspective that cognition is *one important* (and seldom studied) variable in the success and satisfaction of close relationships.

Many books have been written for professionals and for laypersons about marriage and other intimate partner relationships. Sometimes these books are oriented toward the professional marriage or relationship counselor. Sometimes they are written to offer exercises for couples who want to make love last. Some books are explorations of theories, such as attachment theory or learning theory, and how those theories are brought to bear specifically on the conduct of close relationships. So many empirically oriented relationship books and studies are focused on either parent–child relationships or on mate choice and commitment (usually defined as legal marriage).

This book takes a somewhat different approach, by asking cognitive questions about relationships. Although the book rests on a theory that has been the basis for much research and writing, the theory has not been explored extensively *as it applies to relationships*. This book is intended to help fill that gap in understanding. This book opens the exploration to *all* close relationships, including marriage, friendships, sibling relationships, homosexual and heterosexual relationships, and adult parent–child relationships. It explores and addresses relationship dynamics across the lifespan using examples and cases.

The theoretical basis for the book is research on complex postformal thought, which concerns positive cognitive development during adulthood and aging, research I started during my work at the National Institute of Aging/National Institutes of Health (NIA/NIH) and continued afterward over 30 years' time. The book also makes use of the theoretical and empirical work in fields related to close relationships, for example, in attachment theory. My decades of study of complex postformal thought and developmental cognition and their application in everyday life in adulthood have provided groundwork for understanding how the human mind processes information in complex ways and how we solve problems, especially real-life, so-called ill-structured problems. My experience with clients has helped me refine my thinking. Given this background, I have come to the conclusion that it is time to examine more closely how these complex thinking and problem-solving processes are used by individuals to enrich their close relationships and make those relationships more satisfying.

Key purposes of this book, then, include exploring some of the theory and data on *close two-person relationships.* It also is important to begin examining the thinking processes that lead to good or poor relational outcomes for a couple. Finally, there is also a need to construct a research agenda to increase our understanding in these areas.

This book will offer an analysis of the complex thought processes that support relational growth over adulthood. It will provide descriptions of how satisfied close relationship partners think about relationships in all their complexity. It will also suggest areas for future research. In sum, the goals of this book include the following: exploring the theory and data on close two-person relationships; examining some thinking processes that lead to good or poor relational outcomes in a situation; and constructing a research agenda to increase our understanding in these areas.

Since this book offers fresh ideas on cognitive underpinnings of close relationships that thrive, it will not have all the answers to solving relationship problems, nor does it have a cookbook of exercises for relationship partners to use. But it will have suggestions for finding possible answers regarding one very important, yet unexplored, part of what seems to help close relationships work out in a satisfying way.

An Example

Let's see how thinking and problem-solving might help or hinder the experience of a very intractable problem that a couple might experience: they cannot agree on whether or not to have and raise a child.

This is a truly difficult problem for many couples. As you have probably noticed during your own life experience, you cannot compromise on having or not having a child. They don't come in fractional quantities. You can't be a "little bit pregnant," either. And while a dating couple or a newly married couple may have agreed completely at that point in their relationship that they would or would not raise a child, time may alter their opinion on this significant matter. Their personal or couple situation may change over their years together.

There is also a large penalty to pay for one member of the couple forcing a resolution about this on the other member of the couple. Forcing the issue will likely be a prelude to bad feelings, relationship difficulties, power struggles, and paybacks. We can also pity the child, if one is born when one member of the couple hates the idea of having a child. Don't think that this is a rare problem, either. Even if a couple is in agreement at the start of their relationship about having a child, they can develop different perspectives about it later, when some time has passed. This is no one's "fault," since desires and circumstances change for everyone with time and experience.

Here is where problem-solving strategies may become part of the experience. If there is *less* complex problem-solving ability available to the couple, even if the members of the couple are securely attached, loving, mature people, a different process of solving the dilemma will play out than if they had *more* problem-solving ability available to use. Think of cognitive problem-solving ability as if it were money in the bank. Any challenge in life is a little easier to handle with those extra financial resources, to open the field of possibilities a little wider. Maybe you can hire help. Maybe those extra resources will get you a good dinner and a bottle of wine; at least you will *feel* better, your spirits will rise, and you can think of some clever options to solve the problem. The more complex problem-solving strategy available, the more "money in the bank" to help solve the problem at hand.

What strategies does the *less complex* problem-solver have available to think about this problem? Here there are the very limited selections from the "menu," so to speak, of ways this person might approach the dilemma. These characteristics are the opposite of the *postforrmal* complex thought operations, discussed in greater depth in Chapter 2. Instead, they are more like scientific reasoning.

First, the less complex problem-solver could tend toward the more absolute, all-or-nothing kind of response: "It's simple. Are you willing to have a family or not? Which is it? You promised." Notice that a partner who is thinking like this is reasoning in a "scientific thought" sort of way. Promises should be kept. When a "truth" is spoken it cannot be otherwise, or the other partner was lying the first time the couple talked about this and thus was a bad partner from the start. Less complex problem-solvers formulate the situation like a hypothesis statement: If _____, then _____. Period. They think about the process as if it were a philosophical dilemma, or swing to a completely emotional response, ignoring thoughtfulness altogether.

But what if truth is flexible and reality takes on a nebulous quality? Then what is the truth of each other or the relationship? In Chapter 3 the philosophical differences between formal and postformal problem-solving thinking will be linked to scientific approaches, for example, the Newtonian physics vs. quantum physics worldviews. Physicists have had the same formal thought–postformal thought philosophical struggles as they examine the truth of the natural world. Notice how, when thought struggles do not satisfy, even scientists take a "hot" emotional approach and "go with their gut reaction."

A second option is that the less complex problem-solver could try to be the voice of reason and convince the other member of the couple of the "correct" option. "If truth itself is absolute, than I can *make* you see the truth (as I see it) if I just argue forcibly and convincingly. Reasoning (mine) *must* win you over if you are a rational person like me." So, arguments are made for the value, or lack of value, of having that baby, as if there were a single, clearly logical right answer when two reasoning people talk together about deciding to raise children.

Third, the members of this couple might combine the truth of desire for a child with the truth of affection for one another and not be able to separate the two ideas. "If you loved me you would see this my way. If you don't agree (as we did before), you just don't love me. Something's wrong with you as a partner." So if we NOW do not see the same "truth," one of us is not the good, loving person who was in this relationship with me before. Agreement links up with love in this view, as if the two good things or qualities were inseparable. "If we cannot see eye to eye, we MUST not be close emotionally either. So don't worry about the child-raising problem. There IS no real couple relationship here."

A fourth choice on the menu is, of course, to stop trying to solve the problem and just grow more and more distant. This strategy does not really solve the problem. It just creates a new problem of lack of intimacy, draining the relationship of any vitality.

A fifth option is to make this (in abstract terms) an analog-solution type of problem rather than the digital-solution type of problem that it really is. Digital choices involve flipping a metaphorical switch from "yes" to "no" or "off" to "on." Analog choices can fall anywhere on a continuum. Having or raising a child, or not, is an inherently digital type of problem. But the less complex thinker can try to force it into an analog framework by deciding to be a "sort of" halfway parent. This partner doesn't want to break up or fight the other partner into submission, so they half-heartedly agree to what the other person wants. But they remember and semi-consciously hope to settle the score later.

So less complex problem-solvers don't have much to work with in solving complex problems. Since we can't escape life problems during the course of relationships, they may be less likely to experience satisfaction in close relationships, where difficult problems like this one will occur.

Menu Available to the Postformal, Complex Problem-Solver

What are some choices that complex-thinking couples might pick from on their "menu" of choices? Remember, the problem is a disagreement about whether to have or raise a child. As we discussed before, in more abstract terms, this is a digital, not an analog, problem: either they do or they do not raise a child. They can't "sort of" physically be parents.

First, complex-thinking couples can recognize that their partner's point of view may be just as valid as their own. More than one reality may be "true." With this realization they can eliminate blame and being bound by a more rigid reasoning that conflates love with agreement about every important aspect of reality. They can then choose to redefine the conflict in what may be a more resolvable way.

They also get the picture that relationship conflicts of any kind have multiple causes. Even people arguing about something that *seems* clear-cut ("get pregnant or not") may really be arguing about several issues, some of which are largely unconscious. During this discussion it can become clear via a partner that an emotional reality is really at the heart of the conflict. This newly conscious emotional reality might then be resolved, leading to the solution of the originally stated problem.

The complex-thinking couple can also make use of the knowledge that there are likely to be several solutions to any given problem. They can, perhaps, jointly select among the possible solutions to the conflict that reflect a larger reality that encompasses and respects the points of view of both persons.

The complex-thinking couple also can grasp the fact that there are several possible methods they can use to reach a solution to the problem at hand. For example, they may see that deciding to have or not have a child might happen after a fight, or after counseling, or after personal explorations of their motives. All these methods could lead to the same decision. So they can choose one method to pursue, possibly the one that causes the least injury to their relationship.

The complex-thinking couple can also appreciate the paradox of some of their problem-solving situations. For example, although it is not the fastest way, the most useful way to solve the problem of decisions about having children may be to actually spend time exploring their issues, needs, and desires more deeply. In this realization may lie the seeds of the understanding that, although they may not have a solution in hand after today's discussion, they may have found a way to address many different kinds of problems, a generally good process.

The complex-thinking couple will not fall into the destructive habit of expanding the argument into a fight over "everything but the kitchen sink"—in other words, all the various grievances they can think of. They will tend to *define* the problem at hand and set the parameters they want to use to limit the discussion to what is most important for them.

The solution to the original problem of "do we raise a child" might be raised to a reasoning level, to "what do we most want this relationship of ours to be like?" In doing so, they may also find a solution to the original, much narrower problem.

In the next chapter we'll explore complex postformal problem-solving mechanisms. We will also see how close relationships, with their high motivation and emotionality and with their complexity, foster the development of complex postformal thought.

The Development of Complex Thought in Adulthood

Some Theories and Mechanisms that Grow with Interpersonal Experience

P OSTFORMAL THOUGHT IS THE NAME OF MY THEORY, AND POSTFORMAL thought appears to be key to adult development, learning, wisdom, and mature functional, satisfying relationships. It is based on an understanding of reality like that which permeates modern sciences. The concepts and skills of postformal thought derive from cognitive-developmental theory, Native wisdom traditions, "new" sciences such as quantum physics, chaos theory, theories of self-organizing systems, and general systems theory (For more detail on the new sciences, see the Sinnott references cited below.)

Postformal thought is a type of complex logical thinking that develops in adulthood when we interact with other people whose views about some aspect of reality are different from ours. From the background of Piagetian theory (Piaget, 1972; Piaget & Inhelder, 1969; Riegel, 1973, 1975, 1976), lifespan postformal thought builds on concrete and scientific thought categories. It allows a person to deal with everyday reasoning contradictions by letting that person understand that "reality" and the "meaning" of events are co-created with others. Both objectivity and a necessary subjectivity are useful in our epistemological understanding of the world. Postformal thought lets an adult bridge two contradictory "scientifically" reasoning positions and reach an adaptive synthesis of them through higher order logic. The adult then goes on to live the larger reality. So the larger reality eventually *becomes* "true" with the passage of time. Postformal thought includes a necessary subjectivity, which means that the knower understands that "truth" is partially a creation of the one who knows and makes those choices.

Postformal thought uses all the mechanisms identified by cognitive psychology, mechanisms such as memory and attention. It seems to develop later in life, after a certain amount of intellectual and interpersonal experience, according to my earlier research work. For example, only after experiencing satisfying and not-so-satisfying intimate relationships, with their sometimes shared, mutually constructed logics about the reality of intimate life together, can a person be experienced enough to know that "If I think of you as an untrustworthy partner, then treat you that way, you are likely to truly *become* an untrustworthy partner." Postformal thought, or lack of it, has an obvious bearing on the quality of close relationships.

Postformal thinking operations (or skills) also are models of the thinking skills necessary to understand modern scientific approaches such as quantum physics, general systems theory, chaos theory, and theories of self-regulating systems. Postformal thinking skills are needed to allow us to be humanistic, honoring the whole, multifaceted person.

To summarize the argument I am about to make here, postformal thought describes certain cognitive operations. These operations constitute the means for knowing all complex realities like those of modern sciences, such as quantum physics, as well as those in complex emotions and complex human relations.

Why do I believe postformal thought is so central to mature adult thinking and relationships? Why do I think postformal thought is so important for coping with the challenges of the postmodern era? I think these cognitive skills are so essential because over a period of about 30 years of research, I created the theory of complex postformal thought precisely as a way to describe several specific phenomena of this positive sort. I had an ambitious agenda. I wanted to cognitively model the step beyond "formal operational (scientific) logic" (developed in adolescence) and describe the thinking of *mature adult* thinkers. I wanted to cognitively model the *wise* thinking possessed by at least some of my mature relatives, friends, and research respondents. I wanted to cognitively model certain reasoning aspects of the thinking of great twentieth-century scientists such as Albert Einstein. And I wanted to cognitively model some logical aspects of intense, even intimate, long-term *interpersonal interactions that were successful.*

As a university professor, I also saw that I could help students acquire these skills, and that those who had such postformal skills were more successful in their intellectual and interpersonal pursuits. So, since the whole thrust of this research and scholarship was to capture the thinking and learning related to positive outcomes in adult life, I feel confident that the concept of postformal thought is related to, and important to, these significant positive outcomes, and that it should be *developed systematically* in individuals.

Definition and Description of Postformal Thought

Postformal complex thought and the first waves of research underlying it are described in my 1998 book, *The Development of Logic in Adulthood: Postformal Thought and Its Applications* (Sinnott, 1998c). The book outlines the entire theory of postformal thought. Some further references explain this work and the body of theory in which it is nested.

Notice the connections with our topic on satisfaction in relationships. Postformal thought is positively related to some aspects of wisdom (Benovenli, Fuller, Sinnott, & Waterman, 2011). The Postformal Thought Scale is reliable and valid (Cartwright, Galupo, Tyree, & Jennings, 2009) and is a special dimension of older adult problem-solving (Chap & Sinnott, 1977–78). Postformal thought is found in the problem-solving responses of adults from ages 18 to 90, and relates to other cognitive functions (Commons, Armon, Kohlberg, Richards, & Sinnott, 1989; Commons, Richards, & Armon, 1984; Commons & Ross, 2008; Commons, Sinnott, Richards, & Armon, 1989).

Postformal thought is related to development of cross-category friendships (Galupo, Cartwright, & Savage, 2010), as well as to the personality trait of conscientiousness (Griffin et al., 2009). Postformal thought is a separate concept from "intelligence" (Hilton et al., 2013). Postformal thought is also related to *adaptive* acceptance of one's death (Jennings, Galupo, & Cartwright, 2009). Additionally, use of postformal thought facilitates the success of leaders and administrators in international development projects and in the organizational setting (Johnson, 1991,1994, 2004; Johnson & Sinnott, 1996), and "master teachers" use postformal thought (Lee, 1987, 1991, 1994a, b). Postformal thought is positively related to creativity and the ability to hold complex political ideologies (Merchant, 2012).

Postformal thought is related to satisfaction in marital relationships (Rogers, 1989; Rogers, Sinnott, & van Dusen, 1991). Postformal thought is also related to everyday problem-solving ability in adults, to complex gender roles, to social cognition, to clinical transformation, to everyday memory, to solving intragroup workplace conflicts, to emotion, to health, to goal clarity, to family dynamics in dealing with a mental health crisis, to development of spirituality, to adult lifespan learning, to models of lifespan development, to reforming the university as an institution, to teaching professionals in the health professions, to midlife development, to humanistic psychology, to the construction of identity, to positive psychology, to the aging and dying self, to feeing connected with others, to decision-making among older adults, to mindfulness, and to cognitive flexibility (Sinnott, 1975, 1977, 1981, 1982, 1984a, b, 1985, 1986a, b, 1987, 1989a, b, c, d, 1990, 1991a, b, c, 1992, 1993a, b, 1994a, b, c, d, e, 1996, 1997a, b, 1998a, b, c, 1999, 2000, 2001, 2002a, b, 2003a, b, c, 2004a, b, c, d, 2005, 2006, 2007, 2008a, b, 2009a, b, c, d, e, 2010a, b, c, 2011, 2013; Sinnott & Berlanstein, 2006; Sinnott, Block, Grambs, Gaddy, & Davidson, 1980; Sinnott & Cavanaugh, 1991; Sinnott et al., 2013; Sinnott & Guttmann, 1978a, b; Sinnott & Johnson, 1996; Sinnott & Rabin, 2010; Sinnott, Rogers, & Spencer, 1996; Sinnott & Shifren, 2002; Wood, Hilton, Spanos, & Sinnott, 2013; Yan, 1995; Yan & Arlin, 1995).

Note that these references address numerous topics: the reliability and validity of the Postformal Thought Scale; relations between the Postformal Thought Scale and concepts of God, personality, political opinions, and social attitudes; death acceptance and postformal thought; postformal thought and cross-category friendships; creativity and postformal thought; intelligence as measured by standardized tests and postformal thought; intimate relationship satisfaction and postformal thought; community and postformal thought; postformal thought and construction of the self over developmental time; spirituality and postformal thought; postformal thought, expert teaching, and learning; postformal thought and workplace relations; mental health and postformal thought; postformal thought and creative development during personal aging; everyday problem-solving and postformal thought; and postformal thought and reinventing the university. These references also more thoroughly describe the nature and use of the individual thinking operations that together make up postformal thought.

Some of the original work was based on the years of research I performed with the support of the National Institute on Aging (NIA) of the National Institutes of Health (NIH), beginning with my postdoctoral training there. I am grateful to the Gerontology Research Center (GRC) there, and the volunteers of the Baltimore Longitudinal Study of Aging (BLSA) and others who were my research respondents.

An Example

Here is an example of postformal thought in a different type of relationship: When I begin teaching a college class, the class and I begin to structure the reality or truth of our relationship. We decide on the nature of our relationship, act on our view of it, and mutually continue to create it in the days that follow. These various views, held by class members and by me, form several contradictory reasoning systems about the reality of our relationship in the class. One student may see me as a surrogate parent and act within the formal reasoning inherent in that vision, to which I might respond by becoming more and more parental. Another student may logically construct me as a buddy and act within that logical system, to which I might respond by being a buddy too, or by being even more parental to compensate. I might view the class as stimulating or not, and teach in such a way as to make them either. The result over the time of a semester will be an organized "truth" about my relationship with this class that is co-created by the class and me.

While postformal complex thought is *stimulated* by interpersonal interactions among thinkers, once it becomes a thinking tool for a person it may be *applied* to any kind of knowing situation, not just interpersonal ones. I may learn to use the tool of complex postformal thought through interactions with my spouse, and go on to use it to think about Newtonian vs. quantum physics. Just as the tool of scientific reasoning can be used in any context, so too can the tool of complex postformal thought be used in any context. Of course, decisions need to be made about whether it is an appropriate tool in a given context. Complex postformal thought that orders several contradictory reasoning systems is probably less necessary for less epistemologically demanding tasks such as rote memorization of an agreed-upon body of material.

Development of Postformal Thought

The development of postformal thought helps explain how adult college students, for example, change their thinking styles as they go through the university experience. Younger successful students (for example, see the classic study by Perry, 1975) are often concrete thinkers who need to know the "right" answers. They want to know the "right" personality theory and the "right" major for them to study and the "right" way for others to behave. They expect an authority to tell them the answer. Professors temporarily become the authority figures who provide answers. Then, as students proceed through the learning experience, students become relativistic thinkers, shaken by the apparent disappearance of "Truth" ("no right or wrong answers exist"; "there is no way to decide about Truth"; "whatever" [translation: "I don't want to even think about this . . . it is too unimportant or annoying"]). Now they see debates as going on forever, without possible closure. It doesn't matter which philosophy one professes, which major one takes, it's all the same endless, ongoing debate. Finally, students move on to complex thinking, a type of thinking in which they see that a necessary subjectivity is part of decisions about truth. A passionate commitment to the choice of a "reality" leads to making it "real" in the objective world. That complex thinking is what I call postformal thought. At that stage they can say, "It's up to me to pick 'the right major,' then make a commitment to it, act as if it is the 'right' choice for me, and see if it works out. It does matter what I pick . . . not all majors would suit me. But no authority can tell me which will turn out to be 'right.' In fact *no* major will be 'right' unless I commit to it as if some absolute authority told me it is the true major for me."

This complex kind of thinking skill, once attained in any context, can transfer from context to context. The adult student may have gained insight into the complexity of epistemological truth in the context of choosing a major, or in relationships with peers, or as a politician, and go on to use the skill with family members. People start psychotherapy or challenge themselves with difficult growth activities in order to achieve just such a transfer to other areas of their lives. However it is gained, the postformal complex thinker is able to use that set of complex thinking skills in all subject areas and contexts, if he or she chooses to apply it to those contexts.

Two Main Principles

The main characteristics of postformal cognitive operations (Sinnott, 1998b) are (1) self-reference (or "necessary subjectivity") and (2) the ordering of formal operations. *Self-reference* is a general term for the ideas inherent in the new physics (Jones, 1992; Wolf, 1981) and alluded to by Hofstadter (1979), using the terms "self-referential games," "jumping out of the system," and "strange loops." The essential notion of self-reference is that we can never be completely free of the built-in limits of our system of knowing, and *we come to know that this very fact is true*. This means that we somewhat routinely can take into account, in our decisions about truth, the fact that all knowledge has a subjective component and thus is, of necessity, incomplete. So (we conclude) any reasoning we use is self-referential logic. Yet we must *act* in spite of being trapped in partial subjectivity. We make a decision about rules of the game (nature of truth), then act on the basis of those rules. Once we come to realize what we are doing, we then can consciously use such self-referential thought.

The second characteristic of postformal operations is the ordering of formal scientific reasoning operations. The higher level postformal system of self-referential truth decisions gives order to lower level formal truth and reasoning systems. One of these reasoning systems is somewhat subjectively chosen and imposed on data as "true." For example, Perry (1975) describes advanced college students as "deciding" a certain ethical system is "true," while knowing full well that there is no absolute way of deciding the truth of an ethical system.

Looking at another example, relativistic, self-referential organization of several formal operations systems may also be seen. An attorney is trying to decide whether to defend a very young child accused of sexually assaulting another child. There is no conclusive physical evidence and no witnesses were present. Both children are adamant in their stories and both have been known to distort the truth to some degree when they were angry with each other. The attorney must make a commitment to a course of action and follow through on it as if that reasoning system were true. The attorney knows that, when she acts, that reasoning system may become true due to her actions, and will then become legal "truth" in court as well as an emotional truth for her and the others involved.

Formal (scientific) reasoning operations presume reasoning consistency within a single reasoning system. Within that single system the implications of the system are absolute. Postformal operations presume somewhat necessarily subjective selection among logically contradictory formal operational systems, each of which is internally consistent and absolute.

As is true for other cognitive systems, a knower who is capable of using postformal thought skips in and out of that type of thinking. Postformal thought is not always the best way to process a certain experience; it may be that sensorimotor thought (or some other stage of thought) is most *adaptive* on a given day. Perhaps a thinker with higher order thinking skills is being confronted with a new situation for which he or she has no thinking structures to abstract from and no reasoning systems to choose among, not even sensorimotor logic.

For example, a grandparent of mine had never learned to drive, although she was a very intelligent woman. When presented with the chance to learn to drive, the first thing she did was to read about it, trying to use formal thought. Although she knew, after her reading, about "defensive driving" and other concepts like the operation of the automotive engine, these "higher level" skills did not help much when she first tried to engage the clutch and drive away smoothly. In fact, this particular grandmother was so shocked by her first-time, terrible, actual (physical) driving performance, compared to her excellent book understanding, that she began to panic and let the car roll out of control until it came to a stop against a huge rock. Learning the sensorimotor skill of getting that stick shift car out on the road was "lower level" thinking, the most adaptive kind of thinking for that situation. Learning to pick the right level of thought for the occasion may be one thing that people learn is logically possible as they become postformal.

What characterizes the adaptive power of postformal thought? Why is it helpful to an adult? How must adults structure thinking, over and above the operations of formal-operational adolescents, to be in touch with reality and survive? The question here is not about specific facts that need to be known, but rather about general "higher level" intellectual operations, or processes, that the knower needs to master to make existential sense of life and to make life work in situations which go beyond the demands of lower level thinking.

One key thing that competent mature adults seem to need (based on their statements and on observation and task analyses) is to be able to choose one reasoning model (in other words, one formal-operational structure) among the many possible reasoning models to impose on a given cognitive or emotional reality so that they can make decisions and get on with life. They also need to know that they are making necessarily (partly) subjective decisions about reality when they do this.

An ideal context for learning to be a complex thinker is in the course of interactions with others who (whether they intend to or not) challenge our views of reality. Interactions with those we care about too much to simply run away from the argument can be especially powerful in helping us realize the co-created nature of the truths we live.

Postformal Operations of Thought

Nine thinking operations make up my concept of postformal thought. These thinking operations rest on the constructions of interactive reality described by new physics, general systems theory, chaos theory, and theories of dynamic self-regulation systems. Readers who are less interested in the more specific thinking operations that comprise postformal complex thought may want to skip ahead to Chapter 3, where the qualities of these paradigms of interactive reality are discussed in more detail; they seem to me to be important to our deeper understanding of relationship satisfaction. Readers who are less interested in the more specific processes and paradigms offered by the new physics, general systems theory, chaos theory, and dynamic self-regulating systems behavior may want to skip ahead to Chapter 4.

Rationale for inclusion of the operations of postformal thought is given in my summary book about the theory (Sinnott, 1998b). The operations include metatheory shift, problem definition, process/product shift, parameter setting, multiple solutions, pragmatism, multiple causality, multiple methods, and paradox. The references cited earlier in this chapter provide more detail about the meaning of each operation term, the ways these operations have been tested, and the research that provides an underpinning for these assertions. Here I will briefly describe each operation, giving a simple example of each. Note that the operations will relate to one another, but will describe different aspects of the complex thinking process. Note, too, that all the operations relate to problem-solving, in the broadest sense.

Metatheory shift is the ability to view reality from more than one overarching reasoning perspective (for example, from both an abstract and a practical perspective, or from a phenomenological and an experimental perspective) when thinking about it. For example, do I think of my partner as doing the best she can in a complicated situation, or as annoyingly ineffective, or as (of necessity) both?

Problem definition is the realization that there is always more than one way to define a problem, and that one *must* define a problem to solve it, since we all see things like problems through our own unique lenses. For example, I realize that I have to decide, as a partner, whether my goal in this relationship is "talking my partner into having a child" or "deciding together what kind of family life we want, childless or with children," or "ignoring the fact that he is unhappy about our family choices in order to keep things quiet at home." Defining the problem in different ways usually leads to different ways to solve it.

Process/product shift is realizing that one can reach a "content-related" solution to a given problem, and/or a solution that gives one a heuristic or a process that solves many such problems. For example, do I learn how to deal with today's compromise *only*, or do I learn a set of *general* skills for working out compromises in a loving way?

Parameter setting is the realization that one must choose aspects of the problem context that must be considered or ignored for this solution. For example, to have my intimate life AND my work life be healthy and strong (two aspects of life), I will decide to spend time writing, but to limit my writing time today to 2 hours and go home for the afternoon. Just for today I will ignore a third question or aspect: "How am I going to have time for my friends?" All of these decisions and questions set limits ("parameters") for my activity (that is, for my "solution to the problem").

Multiple solutions means that one can generate several solutions, based on several ways to view the problem. For example, I can solve the "problem" of how to have a social life in three ways: do everything together with my partner and her friends; do everything together with my partner and MY friends; or do all my social activities without my partner.

Pragmatism in the case just described means that I am able to evaluate the solutions that I create for this problem, and then select one that is "best" by some definition. *Then* I am able, by some criterion, to use the one that is "best."

Multiple causality is the realization that an event can be the result of several causes. For example, if a friendship fails, I can be aware that it might be due to bad timing (we both have heavy family responsibilities), *and* lack of common interests, *and* my inability to think of what my friend might want.

Multiple methods is the realization that there are several ways to get to the same solution of a problem. For example, the solution to my personal problem, "dealing with my stubbornness in my relationship," may be reached by multiple methods of attack. I can *accept* that I am a stubborn person as well as a kind person, *try to modify* my stubborn traits, or simply see myself as kind and the other person as unworthy of my attention (*polarized position*).

Paradox is realizing that contradictions are inherent in reality, and that the broader view of an event can eliminate contradictions. For example, I see that, paradoxically, starting a family to avoid loneliness may leave me lonelier than before because I will have less time for my friends. In this paradoxical situation, I can only resolve my dilemma by reasoning about it at a more complex level. Perhaps I set a new goal of deciding: "What will give the greatest meaning to my existence in the long run, friends or family?" Only I can decide (self-referential thought) to "jump" to a new cognitive level, or not, to address the question and resolve the paradox.

These individual mental processes, or "operations," are each a part of thinking that I term postformal thought. Taken together, they present the full picture of how such thinking represents the world in full and nuanced ways. The person who can use some of these post-formal operations is able to respond more flexibly to problems than the person who has no use of any of these operations. But the person who can use *all* of them consciously, as the situation calls for their use, can range more widely in finding solutions to life's problems.

The Big Picture

*"New Science" Operations and Logics as a
Way of Understanding Postformal Thought
Operations and Intimate Relationship Processes*

New Physics Models Underlying Postformal Thought

New physics is one of the intellectual ancestors of postformal thought. New-physics thinking is the kind of reasoning thinking structure those complex postformal thinkers—like successful intimate partners, like my wise relatives, and like Einstein—had at their disposal in various forms. The purpose of this discussion is to review some important original ideas basic to the new physics as it was first articulated, that is, as relativity theory and quantum physics. Of course, physics has evolved immensely since the origins of the new physics. But my purpose here is to show how useful even the basic new-physics ideas are as meta-theories for close relationships, especially for cognitive lifespan development. Other post-Newtonian physics paradigms, especially general systems theory, chaos theory, and complexity theories of self-regulating systems, also will be discussed. All of these paradigms reflect elements of basic postformal thought and provide ways to study such thought in the context of relationships.

Far from being frightening or difficult, new-physics ideas are extremely practical when they are applied. These advanced models are being considered in realms as different as spirituality and organization management, and some forms of many of the ideas are apparent in Native American and other indigenous traditions. After all, those concepts must be understandable to us at some level if they can, metaphorically speaking, keep us cognitively dancing in balance on the moving, rotating planet of our reality. These ideas are integral to the universe that is our home.

Historically, we have been accustomed to thinking that our home consists of one room, the layout of which is defined by "old" Newtonian physics. New physics simply opens the door to the rest of the rooms of the house and provides us with the larger floorplan of our home. Like so many moving adventures, once we get accustomed to the new living space, we can't imagine living without it. We move into the postformal larger reality home and think of it as our natural habitat. We become like the child who reaches teen years and can no longer think within the limits of a 6-year-old mind.

The purpose here is to review some of these basic original new-physics concepts to see how they might be used as metaphors to help us understand postformal thought and relationships. New and old physics give us two different ways to describe the apparent same physical reality. Postformal thought permits us to cognitively process both realities at the same time, a cognitive structure that is useful for adaptive lifespan relational development.

Since they are more inclusive, probabilistic and complex, new-physics ideas are difficult to articulate in a verbal system dominated by more rigid functional relations. New-physics ideas would be expected to occur later in the history of any systematic idea development than the simpler and more readily demonstrated earlier ideas. This would be expected in psychology, philosophy, education, sociology, and physics, not because these sciences copy natural sciences, but in spite of the independence of these fields. Scientific advances, whatever the science, take place in a particular historical period and are influenced by the overall tone, predominant thought patterns, and the cultural rules about reality current during that period (Kuhn, 1962; Riegel, 1977). If past history is any guide, new-physics ideas will increase in any period as a function of the number of scientists dissatisfied with any paradigm, the developmental history of the science itself, and the capability of individual scientists to think in such inclusive and probabilistic ways. In sciences or in individuals, new-physics thinking seems to occur because it is adaptive.

To understand the background and concepts of new-physics thought is the first step in its utilization. Interested readers may want to peruse physics textbooks, tap into the huge array of technical books and articles, or scan the very reader-friendly work of writers such as Capra (1975), Jones (1992), Wolf (1981), or Zukav (1979).

Let us look first at the old physics, Newtonian pre-Einstein physics. Classical mechanics had developed as an outgrowth of everyday physical experience with the environment. This experience was first summarized in intuitive and anthropomorphic generalizations, and then in abstract laws. New physics has been developed over a period of years in response to contradictions found while working with the theories of classical mechanics (Russell, 1969). The space of classical mechanics is Euclidian; all transformations in space are describable by Cartesian fixed coordinates and consist of either rotations or translations. Time is an absolute concept, and calculus, presuming continuity of matter and space, is an adequate mathematical tool.

Because of the inability of the scientific observer to become sufficiently objective, measuring standards which appeared to be rigid and absolute were later proved not to be so. To use Einstein's famous example, it was as if the observer were on a speeding train but unaware of its movement. After carefully measuring and describing the environment and relations of objects found while sitting on the train and looking outside the window, the observer would have a certain amount of data. Some of the data would prove shockingly incorrect if the train came to a full stop and the observer were suddenly able to take into account the consequences of motion biases. None of the observer's measures had been wrong for the observer's specific time and place conditions; they simply were not the entire picture of reality. What the observer saw was real data carefully controlled by scientific methodology, but colored by the fact that measurement was not done with a fixed measure but with a changing one (Einstein, 1961).

The scientific or cognitive world of the pre-Einsteinian is like that of the traveler who is still unaware of his or her motion. As we'll see later, developing minds are brought to awareness of their own "motion bias" by interpersonal interactions. The event that brought the awareness of motion bias to the scientist was work in electromagnetism. As a result of discoveries in that field, phenomena at variance with Newtonian physics were discovered. Newton, for example, held that only the distance between two objects determined the strength of forces they exerted upon one another. This was contradicted by Oersted's work, demonstrating that relative motion is also important in determining object interaction, and by Maxwell, who demonstrated field effects' importance in the strength of forces between bodies. Attempts to deal with these contradictions led to the new mathematical tools of vector analysis and tensor analysis, to Einstein's elaborations on relativity theory and to quantum mechanics. Contradictions led to a new physics.

Postulates

The postulates of relativity theory in new physics are simple to express but difficult to conceptualize. Observers fail to recognize that their standards of measurement of events are *not* truly rigid (i.e., consistent or absolute) ones unless they deal with small-scale, isolated limiting case events. The *first postulate of relativity* is valid only for such limiting cases: If, relative to K, K′ is a uniformly moving system of coordinates devoid of rotations, K and K′ share the same natural laws (Einstein, 1961). In other words when two persons are both on the train, their scientific, objective findings agree with one another. The problem, as might be expected, comes when K and K′ are not uniformly moving systems of coordinates devoid of rotation, that is, when both observers are not on the same train. When one goes beyond the somewhat reductionistic small-scale descriptions of nature, not every observer can be on the train.

The *second postulate*, or the *special theory of relativity*, was formulated in response to this type of problem and contradiction in data. In the second postulate, certain formerly rigid concepts such as time and space are made dependent on the motion (or non-motion) of the reference body. The Lorentz transform (Einstein, 1961) was developed as a mathematical tool for moving from one system of positional coordinates to another, to allow for the effect of shifting vantage points. According to this postulate, general laws of nature may still be deduced from such idiosyncratic experiences, *if* their coordinate systems are related by the Lorentz transform. In other words, if the space/time position on the train can be related to the space/time on the road, a general law which applies to both locations can be determined.

The *general theory of relativity*, or the *third postulate*, was formulated to replace Newton's theory of gravity, which would be impossible under this new set of assumptions, with an explanation consistent with the new set of assumptions. The inseparable space/time dimension of one body was coordinated with the dimension of nearness-to-another-body. The result was that a graphic description of space/time took on a curvature. In other words, when two bodies approach one another, the closer they get, the more their paths in space/time deviate from a straight line. The closer a moving train approaches the top of a mountain, the slower and more circular its path. The mathematics of moving a vector like the train from place to place without changing its size or orientation (i.e., the mathematics of "parallel transport") was developed to deal with movement in space/time across a curved surface. Assuming that objects travel the most efficient route from point to point, this new tool allows one to describe space/time movement in spite of the gravitational field. It therefore allows transformation of coordinate systems even when such transforms are multidimensional and continuous. The general theory of relativity demands that a natural law be applicable to multidimensional, continuous transforms of coordinate systems, if it is to be a *general* law (Einstein, 1961).

Pre-Einsteinian theories include laws of nature which appear general, but which are general only under certain specific reductionistic space/time conditions. Einstein's laws of nature include Newton's as special cases.

Assumptions

Many assumptions characterize old physics and differ from those in new physics. We will highlight just a few of these and examine them. Note that both sets of assumptions have been verified with experimental evidence, so both contradictory sets of assumptions are true. Newtonian physics assumptions have been found to be true in small-scale, everyday systems, except for minor inconsistencies; new-physics assumptions are true for the general case and include the others as special limiting conditions.

SPACE

The nature of space differs between the two sets of assumptions (Kaufman, 1973). Space can be described as Euclidean when the measuring standard is at rest, the limiting case. Space must be described as non-Euclidean in the general case. In the former situation, the shortest distance between two points is a straight line, while in the latter, it is a geodesic (i.e., a curved path describing the shortest distance between two points located on a curved surface). Aristotelian logic appears challenged by the destabilization of concepts such as space and time, and by the allowance of reasoning contradiction in terms of limiting case postulates vs. general case postulates.

CONTINUITY

An assumption under Newtonian physics and the calculus which it utilized is the continuity of phenomena—time, place, events—which are assumed to be isolated, measured against rigid standards, and ordered in an unchanging manner. Under the new set of assumptions, phenomena are continuous only in the limiting case, but discontinuous in general (Robertson & Noonan, 1968).

The absolute nature of time and space in the pre-Einstein perspective is replaced by the space/time interval (Einstein, 1961). The interval allows the effect of time on space, or of space on time, to be taken into account when locating an event or reasoning about it. As events approach the speed of light, time slows down. An event which is simultaneous with another event (in one view) also precedes that event (in a second view) and is subsequent to it (in a third view). On the other hand, if the time element is variously measured, the position of the event in space may assume several contradictory sets of coordinates for the same event.

The conceptualization of the uniformity of space also changes (Russell, 1969). In the former metatheory, space is uniform throughout; in the latter, space appears filled with hills and valleys which offer greater and lesser resistances to moving bodies. These gravitational fields, that is, the hills encountered, slow the moving body and make its path more circular, allowing it to approach but never attain the center of the field.

MOVEMENT

Two observers can never reach valid conclusions about the same event if they fail to take their own movement into account (Brillouin, 1970). What the two observers see at a given time would be determined by their motion relative to one another and to the event. Using the train example, if one person on the road and a second on the moving train see a star, the reality of their physical relation to the star can only be ascertained after the effect of the motion of the earth, the motion of the train, and the motion of the star are taken into account. The formulation of a scientific hypothesis, that is, an epistemology or a knowing of the relations between oneself and the star, is incomplete if it does not develop beyond pre-Einsteinian notions. In other words, if one attempts to know the star in terms of physical experience in Newtonian physics terms, one will lack a complete understanding of the star in a larger sense. The lesser knowledge may be sufficient for some situations, but not for all situations. An additional abstraction from abstractions must be made, one which permits egocentrism in a sophisticated sense in which one always takes one's biases into account. Both the small-scale principles of physical relations, which are useful every day, and the general-scale multiple vantage points principles of physical relations, which are the more inclusive assessment, must coexist in thinking, contradictory as they seem to be, to know reality in all its forms and to adapt to different situations. Postformal thought gives us the cognitive framework for doing so.

CAUSALITY

Conceptions of causality are broadened in new-physics thought (Toulmin, 1970). The deterministic causality of Newtonian physics is enlarged by the deterministic probabilistic causality of quantum mechanics (Heisenberg, 1958; Schlick, 1970). Simple Newtonian deterministic physical causality would pertain in limited situations and would assume contiguity (i.e., cause and effect necessarily in contact). A *new-physics* definition of causality, in contrast, could be "a timeless relation of dependency between two events," or "a center around which events (i.e., effects) are grouped." The relatedness of two specific events in a limited fixed space/time can be predicted on a simple, deterministic basis, but the general relatedness of two events only can be predicted on a complex, probabilistic basis. The implications of this for the scientific method have been vast. While the new student of science may still look for simple experimental "cause and effect relations," the advanced investigator is now more likely to focus on chaos and complexity theory, self-organizing systems, and the implicit order as he or she thinks about causes.

Causality is determinable within a relativistic system, but the limits bounding those determinants are much wider than they are in simpler systems. Ideas of non-local causation and the paradox of Schrödinger's cat certainly intrigue us. Relativistic thinking seems more ecologically valid for explaining effects and causes in a naturalistic setting where many variables are in constant interplay. Looking at the Newtonian micro-universe of the developing fetus, for example, one chemical change does determine a specific limiting case reaction. More important, though, is the overall general new-physics reaction of the fetus, which is determined not only by the chemical, but probabilistically also by the prevailing fetal milieu and history. The chemical, in the general case, is simply the center of a complex but predictable response. Later writers have examined such concepts as "non-local causality" in physics in general (e.g., Bohm, 1980), as well as in biology (e.g., Sheldrake, 1981, 1989, 1990), and medicine.

Subjectivity and Linguistic Transform Systems

The concept of egocentrism comes full circle through transition from the prescientific ego-boundedness of the child, through supposed objectivity of the young adult, to the new-physics notion that the data and the observer are in an *ongoing necessary interaction*. In the third stage, the person who attempts to be decentered and objective learns that subjectivity must be made part of the measure of the phenomenon itself, and that objective reality is better defined as the sum of observational invariants, even though each of those invariants is known to be necessarily partly subjective (Born, 1962, 1964).

But there is a catch. The logic and laws of nature have been formulated within verbal conventions that make it difficult to understand this new physics objectivity in a non-polarized way. For example, present-tense declarative verbal statements fit Aristotelian logic but would not fit new-physics general-case ideas well (Freedle, 1977). The "either A or non-A" forms in language usage are also basically old physics, making expressions of new physics ideas (e.g., "both A and non-A") seem contradictory. No wonder mathematicians or lovers sometimes avoid words.

Large-Scale Developments

Perhaps one of the most interesting issues integral to this thought transition in physics has concerned the nature of the universe and its development over time (Kaufman, 1973). Newtonian-physics thought conceptualizes the universe as uniform and existing in a stable state. This was philosophically consistent with early views of human nature and creation (Russell, 1969). In new-physics terms, the universe has proved to be non-uniform, with some portions more densely filled with matter while others are more nearly empty space. These fuller and emptier portions of the universe are in motion relative to one another. The new-physics view can accommodate three types of universe. Either the universe is continuously expanding and becoming less dense, or the universe is continuously creating and destroying itself, or parallel universes exist.

A new-physics pattern of relations among elements in the universe, applied to individual development or to social interactions, suggests that development might be either continuous differentiation or an alternating process of pattern creation and destruction. Perhaps readers can envision others. Using relations in the new-physics universe as an analog, development would *not* likely be the attainment of any long-term steady, unchanging mature state among individuals or within individuals.

Applications to Lifespan Developmental Psychology

Can some parallels and analogies be constructed between old-physics or new-physics concepts and concepts in lifespan developmental psychology? Do we see evidence of one or the other physics or both, indicating a time of transition? Psychology seems to be struggling with the situation that we know many facts but relatively few general laws. Simultaneous reliable measurements of the same event are producing different and contradictory interpretations when viewed from the small-scale and the large-scale perspectives. Measures fail to yield deterministic results in ecologically valid situations. We are increasingly interested in multivariate relations that have nonlinear forms. This frame of mind suggests that we are in a transition state or a paradigm shift in psychology.

Several relationships studied by lifespan developmentalists are analogous to relationships in the physical sciences.

Postulate Applications

In model terms, early work in lifespan development seems to have been concerned with clarification of the first postulate described here. Investigators have been expected to choose a limiting case perspective and stay with it. Choice of several paradigms or referents has been considered evidence of reasoning inconsistency, as indeed was true of Aristotelian logical views of logical consistency. For example, the organism had to be considered either active or passive, not both, in Aristotelian terms. Within classical mechanics, analogously, a great deal of effort was once spent to describe light definitively as either a wave or a particle only to conclude that light really was both.

Studies in psychology examining cross-cultural differences, longitudinal vs. cross-sectional studies, and demands for contexted personality and intelligence measures suggest that psychology is becoming aware of the second postulate and its analogs for human behavior and noting how both the subject and the observer are in motion. When time and space are viewed as discrete, the organism seems to change as a function of either time (age alone, the maturational perspective) or space (experience alone, the behaviorist perspective). Instead of acrimonious debates, if the organism could be viewed as moving across space/time intervals during its development, many contradictions could be resolved.

The simple transformations of time and space which apply to the limited case of the old physics are replaced by the complex *new-physics transforms* which describe relative position in developmental space/time of interaction individuals and environmental factors. This tedious, polarized language can be replaced by a formula or a graphic that better conveys the larger new-physics picture: two grids have elastic dimensions, those dimensions influenced by past and present relations with one another. At any moment, the relation of one grid to another can be calculated. That relationship, rather than their comparative ages or the simple distance between them, is the most useful thing one could know to predict how (or whether) the grids will be alike, how much they will gravitate toward one another or repel each other, or how alike they will be in relation to other variables or grids. Using these concepts, one can explore the effects of the developmental histories and environments of social individuals on their individual growth and behavior.

For example, it may be true for infants that age (time) is isolatable as a determinant of much of neurological development. It may be true for 7-year-olds that experience (an analog of space) with the written word is an isolatable determinant of reading proficiency. But a "space/time (experience/age) interval" seems to be more useful in describing the larger developments (motions), such as social development and adult development. The position of a developing individual seems to be most adequately conceptualized as an age/experience point in motion, a point that can be described as vector-like and potentially analyzed as such. The coordinated systems of two developing individuals at any point might be considered as if individuals were located on grids of differing proportions, grids which could be related only by transforms. Only in small-scale cases (i.e., those which take place within a short time or within a limited space) could the positional data for one individual be directly related to the positional data for the other, because under those circumstances both occupy the same grid ("are on the same moving train").

In view of these ideas, whatever measuring standard is used in lifespan development can be a rigid standard only on the small-scale basis. One's past scores are a rigid standard measuring the same thing each time only if very little time or experience has passed; one would not have the same testing device in hand after 20 years of personal experience has altered the meaning of that device for the test-taker. Attempts to make measuring devices rigid frequently make them meaningless or ecologically invalid.

As Riegel (1977) noted, even though the lifespan represents an ongoing time sequence, researchers persist in viewing it in frozen or rigid segments. Perhaps some psychologists freeze these segments of experience because they communicate and think in polarized language. Yet, those segments of the lifespan are fluid because they are in constant motion; what they are today is not what they are tomorrow. We observers are moving through our own lifespans, and what we measure against today (i.e., the meaning we give symbols today) is not what we measure against tomorrow. Riegel stressed the importance of looking at contradictions in frozen segments over time, because those contradictions certainly are one measure of space/time. The task remains to find a manner of transforming the sets of space/time coordinates so that each set is understandable in terms of the other when both are undergoing constant change due to both their development and interaction. The transforms needed may ultimately resemble Fourier transforms, and the task of communication of this information may ultimately resemble that of psychoneuroimmunological communication.

The third postulate appears especially applicable to the behavioral sciences, since those sciences study not only the development of a single individual in a physical world, but the development of an individual who is interacting with other developing individuals. In an attempt to "stop the moving train" and to make measures rigidly stable, the effect of developing individuals on each other is often put aside. Besides raising questions about the ecological validity of the resulting findings, the compartmentalization of all social development into a few studies seems to have largely isolated such studies from what could be useful cognitive and intraindividual developmental analysis (Kuhn, 1978).

Developmentalists are fortunate when they become aware that the Newtonian-model separation between the social and the individual spheres of influence is simply an arbitrary device used by one paradigm. The effect of a moving body on another moving body was, in Newtonian physics, isolated and examined as a separate physical phenomenon (gravity), since Newtonians did not know that this separation was an artificial one. Developmentalists behave like Newtonians when relationships between developments on adjacent bodies are overlooked or when psychological nearness of developing entities is ignored. This earlier paradigm weakness may have been one of the main stumbling blocks in moving from specific laws of development to general laws of development in the past.

How might developing individuals mutually affect one another in terms of analogs of the third postulate? In relativistic terms, they might change the shape and the dimensions of each other's developmental space/time and affect the direction of each other's movement. Development may fairly be visualized as a straight-line function in a small-scale event. But, over the life course, it is not fair to do so. We notice that the direction and speed of lifespan development is often changed by encounters with persons and events that the individual later perceives as important. The first others encountered have stronger deflecting action than later ones, just as planets caught in each other's gravitational fields remain influenced by that first encounter, unless changes within the planet itself or the passing of a stronger third body are the occasion for changing relationships. The interaction with developing others encountered during one's own development probably, in natural science terms, describes a geodesic. One continually approaches, circles, and is repelled by the other, but one has been permanently deflected and is constantly affected by the other's nearness. The impact is also mutual. Interpersonal space during development can then be described as a hilly surface with each individual as the top of a hill, and all the hills in motion through space/time. As each gets nearer to knowing or influencing the other, resistance increases, so that a slowing circular motion carries the approaching ones around each other. If one were to step close to the surface of one of those hills, one body actually making giant circles around another would seem to move straight ahead; local small-scale events appear non-relativistic and separable into individual developments and social developments.

The new-physics view of social interaction has implications for understanding social development, emotional growth, peer pressure effects, group dynamics, and dynamics of successful therapy, to name a few. In considering, for example, whether a person will succumb to peer pressure to cheat, a researcher can predict cheating on the basis of such variables as the need to conform, past history of tax evasion, moral code, etc. If the researcher is using a new-physics meta-theory, the researcher would be less interested in specific factors predicting cheating and more interested in the cheating as one point in the person's movement through developmental space/time, a part of encounters with other developing persons sharing that domain. A particular person may appear to conform to pressure but, from a larger perspective, is actually within the gravitational pull of a significant relationship that carries important shared-meaning transforms equating cheating with independence or some other positive trait. The most important benefit of this analysis is not the more accurate prediction of cheating but the ability to understand the complex course of development.

Postmodern Thought and Other Practical Consequences of New-Physics Models

Postmodern thought, also known as postpositivist and post-Enlightenment thought, seems to flow from new-physics realizations. The postmodern perspective challenges positivist assumptions that reason can provide us with a truly objective view of truth and that science is neutral in terms of the lenses through which it views reality. Postmodernists also question the existence of a stable and coherent "self," a self which possesses a language that truly captures objective reality. Within postmodernism are social constructionism and deconstruction views. The former states that the knowledge we have of something is a constructed representation, not a replica, of reality. Deconstructionists (or poststructuralists) see language as a social construct for representing and simultaneously, necessarily, distorting reality. These views help reframe questions along new-physics lines in many of the humanities and social sciences.

We have outlined just a few of the concepts in the new physics that have tremendous potential for models of lifespan development. Additional extremely important ideas might be explored, ideas such as Bohm's (1980) concept of implicate and explicate order, superstring theory, antimatter, and unified field theories. But staying within the few key concepts we have explored so far, those from the early part of the history of the new physics, what are the practical implications of several of those concepts for lifespan developmental psychology?

In the small-scale study, nothing would change except the awareness that the laws obtained through reductionistic (in the sense of Newtonian-level physics) analyses apply only to small-scale situations, not to the general picture of development. Description of general laws, in contrast, would begin by viewing all measures to some degree as projectives. All events would be considered in terms of their meaning to the individuals that participate in them, and the consensus among individuals concerning meaning would constitute the invariant of the events, the portion perceivable by *all* participants, whether they are (metaphorically speaking) "on" or "off" a given train. No stages of development would be sought in describing general laws, and age alone would not be meaningful. The major objects of inquiry would be the direction, the rate, and the quality of developmental change. The vectors of two developing individuals would be related by means of appropriate transforms, and interpersonal studies would be based on "nearness of the other" effects. Direction, rate, and quality of developmental change would be symbolically translatable from individual to individual; direction, rate, quality, and nearness would characterize groups of interacting individuals and would also be symbolically translatable. The time dimension would become a part of the symbol; other persons and society would also be part of the symbol, not just factors to be controlled. Results would be visualizable on other than flat, two-dimensional surfaces. The subject and object of experimental relationships would be inseparable, as would intrapersonal and social dimensions of any event. Rate, quality, and direction of development would be continuous in the individual until the termination of the group. Events would neither be indeterminate nor determinable from *single* causes; instead, the limits of possible determinates would be enlarged.

The practical consequences of exploring this meta-theory would include, but not be limited to, the following:

Continuation of studies describing stages and age effects, with awareness that they are valid only for the limited case situation

Graphic or mathematical descriptions of the developmental life course, which would include integration of biological, social, historical, interpersonal and other psychological events, with development of new research strategies and tools

Deeper understanding of the effects of social experience, especially early social experience

Desolution of conflicts among many models

Understanding of conflicts among individuals

Techniques for describing social development across the lifespan in a cognitive and interpersonal context, and for describing the development of social groups

Better understanding of what is shared in verbal communication, how it can be shared, and the nature and limits of the verbal transform system

New approaches to the nature and experience of adult development

> Growth in studies focused on postformal thought and on the epistemology of new-physics thought, including the relation of use of postformal thought to adaptation

The last point mentioned, the growth of studies focused on post-formal thought and on the epistemology of new-physics thought, including the relation of use of postformal thought to adaptation, is one of great importance. As Cassirer (1923, 1950, 1956) writes, there is a sort of spiritual community between physics and epistemology that has been continuing a fruitful dialogue during the ongoing for-mulation of relativity and quantum theories. We are seeing in this book how this spiritual community may bear fruit in the under-standing of human behavior and development, especially the cogni-tive and interpersonal development linked to postformal thought and wisdom.

General Systems Theory Underlies Postformal Thought

The second, newer model or set of theories that underlies my theory of postformal thought is general systems theory, or as we can affec-tionately call it, GST. Developed hand in hand with the new phys-ics and biology, GST is useful for students of adult development and especially adult cognitive development. It offers ways to think about complex system interactions—not only interactions among suppos-edly inert physical systems (the focus of physics) but also among *liv-ing* systems.

The reasons we are discussing these views of the world in this particular book are twofold. First, since they are the ancestors or underpinnings of the theory of postformal thought, knowing more about them should help you, the reader, understand and evaluate the theory of postformal thought. Second, scientists, philosophers, and humanists are turning increasingly to world views such as these to describe how twentieth-century humans construct their world and give their lives meaning. Yet many well-educated professional adults have not had the chance to become acquainted with one or the other of these views. In the course of this chapter, I hope to share with you what I take to be the most important principles of GST. In later chap-ters we will apply these principles as we apply postformal theory to problems of adult development.

GST is an *amusing* theory. In a lecture, the physicist Wigner once said that theories can be "interesting" or "amusing." An interesting theory may have merit, but often such theories are quickly forgotten; an amusing theory is a theory that makes one *think* and play with the possibilities. GST is an amusing theory.

GST, as I shall use the term here, is an attempt to unify science by finding structures and processes common to many entities. Of greatest interest are entities which are complex organizations that have boundaries, have some continuity over time, and are able to change in orderly ways over time. Such entities may be called living systems (Miller, 1978), whether they are cells or societies or some other type of entity. Among the earlier theorists of GST are such luminaries as Norbert Weiner (1961), Ludwig von Bertalanfy (1968), and Blauberg, Sadovsky, and Yudin (1977). Today GST is expressed in the language of quantum physics, chemistry, the many family systems approaches in clinical psychology, game theory (von Neumann & Morgenstern, 1947), biofeedback, sociology (Lockland, 1973), and many other disciplines (Mahoney, 1991). The growth of interest in systems views is due in part to the growth of knowledge that prods us to go beyond singe-variable studies to complex expressions of relationship and process. We also have new ways to analyze such complex systems data, and when tools exist, uses for them are created. Of course, that statement itself is a systems theory interpretation of these events over time.

What are some of the core themes of GST? The first is the concept of a *system*, that is, a network of related components and processes that work as a whole. *Linkage* and *interaction* are key themes, because whatever influences one part or process influences all of the parts and processes, that is, influences the entire system. Systems coordinate their activities by means of *feedback*, either from within or without. Feedback from within leads to homeostasis or equilibrium within; feedback from without leads to balance between two or more systems. *Equilibrium* is a balance between or among system parts. Given a state of disequilibrium, there will be an energy flow from one part to another. Any number of systems can have common mechanisms (*isomorphic processes*) for doing some task. For example, getting energy from one point to another may occur by means of chemical transmission or glucose metabolism, or by moving commuters via subways in a "city system." Because systems do interact and trade things such as energy, GST recognizes that scientists need to make deliberate decisions to specify system limits or parameters and levels of description. We have not always done this in the past. Thus, there is an awareness of the observer's input on the "reality" observed, an emphasis reminiscent of the new physics. For example, if I draw living-system boundaries at the person level, I may correctly say that a middle-aged woman's depression is due to poor coping strategies; if I draw the boundaries at the societal living-system level, I may argue with equal correctness that the depression is caused by social stigmas attached to women aging. I would be correct in both cases but would investigate different things.

Systems theory examines multiple causal variables, or at least considers that they may be present, and focuses most on the processes used to go from one state to another. This makes GST a "natural" for developmental psychologists, such as me, who are interested in the multidetermined processes behind changes over time as much as in the states of persons at various time points. GST as a worldview is interested in both the melody and the chords of any life song.

What are some systems functions that are commonly present in all systems? First, a "living" (in the broad sense used before) system operates so as to *maintain some continuity over time*, some structured wholeness, even while continuing, if appropriate, to grow. Second, systems function to *contain and transfer energy and information* from one point to another, within or between them. All systems have some means of *boundary creation* and maintenance, as well as means of *interaction with other systems*. This implies that the boundary must be permeable, to some extent, but not so permeable that the system will merge with other systems. Other systems functions are to *control processes, run circular processes*, and *give feedback*. The overall goal is to provide optimum input for continuity and growth, while avoiding pathological abnormalities and *maintaining flexibility*.

Systems do change over time. How does this happen? The only way systems can change over time is if some entropy or disorder is present. If this is counterintuitive, consider for a moment what would happen if no disorder were present and all elements were structured into some form: there would be no space available and no raw material to use to make new forms. For example, if a child used all available blocks to make a toy city (i.e., all the blocks were "ordered"), some disorder would have to be introduced (e.g., push the blocks into a pile on the side) to make room for the next orderly structure (perhaps a large house) to be built. If my mind is made up about an issue, I must introduce doubt before a change of mind is possible. So disorder (entropy) is not only the catastrophic final state predicted by the second law of thermodynamics but also the beneficial means to a flexible reordering and growth to a larger order.

When systems change over time, they usually move from complete disorder or potential through increasing order and bounding to a relative balance between order and potential, a state that may last most of the system's "lifetime." As systems "die" they move toward rigidity, which is a state of very low potential and overwhelming order. All the system's decisions have been made already, so to speak; all its choices are over. The overly ordered, overly structured rigid state admits no change and will be shattered by any input from outside. An analogy is what happens to a rigid crystal goblet that breaks under high-frequency vibrations, whereas the even thinner skin on the hand holding it does not. Prigogene (1980) notes that it is always possible to create a better structure by shattering a rigid state. From that shattering and the availability it creates will come a more flexible, more complex form. This means the death of the old system, or its reemergence in *very* altered form.

Imagine a situation in which two systems (societies, for example) come up against each other and try to influence each other, that is, they intrude on each other's boundaries. If the first system is not too rigid and too ordered, the influence and energy of the second will have an impact and alter the first. The reciprocal will also be true. But if the first system is rigid, the second will not influence it easily. It will have to try harder, if it can. Let's say the intruder system does try harder still. If it cannot influence the rigid first system subtly, the more violent influence it may resort to may result in a complete shattering of the first system. The first system did not "go with the flow," "co-opt the opposition," or "make a deal." For a rigid system in which compromise is out of the question, every fight with a worthy opponent is a fight to the death. What a high price to pay for necessary and ordinary adaptations.

The gentler dynamic—mutual influence of semi-ordered systems—occurs during non-loaded discussions by members of a couple. The second, more catastrophic dynamic—destruction of an old overly rigid system—occurs during catastrophic clashes by members of a couple who can no longer communicate.

System change over time, therefore, demands a significant degree of entropy. But systems resist disorder on any large scale, and change means the temporary elimination of much order. The resistance to disorder in the psychological system is evident in the sometimes painful reorganizations during personal change, for example, change during psychotherapy or during crises. Any system tries to monitor and control the extent of disorder, but hopes not to need to resist absolutely, because that would take too much energy. Surviving systems balance their potentials and actualizations, have boundaries but are not closed entirely, try to fit many contexts flexibly, and attempt to interface with other systems without being engulfed or engulfing. Non-surviving systems may have the same structures (e.g., a boundary) but may have different processes (e.g., *rigidity* in a boundary) that are less adaptive.

Chaos, Complexity, Self-Regulating Systems, and Postformal Thought

The ideas of chaos theory, complexity theory, self-regulating systems, and new biology are additional ways to describe complex interactions. These also arise from physics to some extent, but are grounded even more strongly in computer science and biology. They are all useful as worldviews or methods for the study of lifespan cognitive postformal development and thus for its application to the complexity of close relationships.

The processes described by new physics, GST, chaos, complexity, self-regulating systems, and new biology can be deeply understood only by the postformal reasoning thinker because they often violate the core linear logic of the formal operational hypothetico-deductive scientific thinker. This is one reason these new sciences seem hard to grasp and hard to teach in the average high school or college physics class. Granted, a student can repeat back axioms of a science even if he or she does not understand them, but that is not deep understanding. The individual with deep understanding can use the concepts to creatively solve problems. Something very much like postformal thought is necessary to deeply *understand* these new science ideas, provided, of course, the thinker has the chance to become familiar with the jargon. If some "postformal adult logic" had not already been described by those of us who are studying it, something like it would have to be invented to describe the thinking processes of the creators of these new science fields. They seem to be postformal thinkers. At an epistemological level, the postformal thinker can choose a way to know the complexities of the world. Those complex choices seem to frame the world in some of the same ways that chaos theory and the other new sciences frame it.

I examined these new science ideas to see more of the logical thought processes that let humans think this advanced way, to get some feeling for the next stage (after formal thought) of cognitive development, and to obtain a wider view of philosophies and world-views in which postformal thought and its co-created reality could fit comfortably. This is especially important to the development of close relationship interactions.

What Is Chaos Theory?

Chaos theory is a new mathematical model that has been used in the last two decades to describe phenomena as different as weather, the structure of coastlines, brain wave patterns, adult learning, normal or abnormal heartbeat patterns, family transitions, the behavior of the mentally ill, intractable conflict, and much, much more (Alper, 1989; Cavanaugh, 1989; Cavanaugh & McGuire, 1994; Crutchfield, Farmer, Packard, & Shaw, 1986; Gleick, 1987; Gottman, 1991; Pool, 1989; Sinnott, 1990; Vallacher, Coleman, Nowak, & Bui-Wrzosinska, 2010). General and lengthier descriptions of chaos theory are available in Abraham (1985), Barton (1994), Devaney (1989), Gleick (1987), Goerner (1994), Levine and Fitzgerald (1992), and Smith and Thelan (1993). Chaos theory describes the orderly and flexible nature of apparent disorder. It mathematically describes complex systems with nonlinear equations. It describes commonalities of *processes* over time which would otherwise appear *dis*orderly if viewed at one time point.

KEY CONCEPTS

Chaos theory works with dynamical systems, which are systems in which the contents of the system and the processes of the system mutually influence each other. In such systems, the current state of the system is fed back to it before it makes another iteration or goes through another round of changes. The system then repeats its process, each time with updated information. Such systems tend to begin to appear stable over time.

But such systems are deterministic, as well as unpredictable, with only the appearance of stability. The behavior at each iteration is not predictable, but the limits built into the system confine it in predictable ways. So there is a "hidden" order that also gradually emerges from beneath the disorder. Chaotic systems somewhat resemble the rambling pattern of footprints made by a curious dog on a very long leash: at first there seems to be no pattern, but soon, after enough walking, a pattern emerges. Part of that emergent pattern is centered on the leash and on what or whoever is holding it; that part is truly deterministic. Part of what emerges is specific to the next part of the dog's rambling walk; that part is unpredictable.

One striking feature of chaotic systems is the way in which they explain why a tiny disturbance or "perturbation" can lead to complete rescaling of the entire pattern of the system due to structural instability. This has been termed the "butterfly effect" (Lorenz, 1963, 1979), because weather forecasters using computer models have seen the "breeze" from a butterfly moving its wings (some idiosyncratic perturbation) eventually lead to a whole new direction of wind movement, even though the overall pattern of the actual wind was not changed by the creators of the computer model. Dynamical systems are generally structurally unstable, demonstrating these large impacts from small changes. However, it is possible for them to be stable. We humans certainly prefer to think of things as structurally stable and thus "find" stability even where little exists.

Another feature of chaotic systems is the way a seemingly random set of events, after many repetitive interactions, can coalesce around a point in an apparently orderly way. The impression is of a dominant feature of some sort, analogous to a dominant personality trait or a hurricane eye. This phenomenon is termed a "strange attractor" because the point looks like it pulls in the events around it.

It sometimes helps to think of chaos as organized disorder, as opposed to sheer randomness, or *dis*organized disorder. In orderly disorder, a flexible structure is hidden in events that only seem to be driven by change when examined in linear or one-time slices. The hidden order unfolds gradually to make itself known when the longer term nonlinear pattern is observed. In true randomness, or *disorderly* disorder, there is no hidden underlying structure. Without some chaotic flexibility, some orderly readiness to fluctuate built into the system, a system (especially one like the heart or brain) is too rigid to adapt and live. For example, a rigid heartbeat pattern (no chaos) cannot effectively and efficiently correct for a small perturbing error like a skipped beat, so a heart attack occurs. A rigid brain wave pattern cannot respond effectively to an intellectual challenge, so poor performance results.

Chaotic disorder is non-random and has a kind of potential to correct for errors by the use of the underlying, hidden corrective mechanism of the basic, deeper pattern. Chaos is an order enfolded into apparent disorder; it is the pattern in the hologram, akin to the "implicate order" described by Prigogene and Stengers (1984). Implicate order means that an orderly message is encoded within the surface and the apparent disorder, so that the implied message can be unfolded and read. Genetic material is another example of this implied message, which is unpacked, decoded, and read by the organism as the organism develops from its first cells to its full hereditary potential. But the unfolding makes even a very minor element powerful enough to create major effects.

Chaos theory provides a rationale for synchronous effects, those apparently unrelated events that seem to mysteriously occur together. The synchronous systems demonstrate entrainment, in which one system locks onto the mode and pattern of another nearby system. The minor event in one system then can move the other system with it.

Chaos models have interesting ways of describing the mechanisms of abrupt or qualitative change. For example, a thinker can move from seeing the world with concrete reasoning to somewhat suddenly (an "aha" reaction) seeing the world with formal logic. When a thinker suddenly begins to see the world in formal operational terms (whereas before the world was framed in concrete operational terms), many kinds of behavior are affected. Bifurcation models within chaos theory seem to describe this kind of sudden shift event. In a bifurcation model, at first possibilities (actually possible equation solutions) emerge from one point, like branches on a young sapling tree. But later in the tree's progression through time, the newest branches seem to cluster around several source points, not just one, with young branches coming off two or three more major limbs, going in different directions. This shift from one group of possibilities to several groups of possibilities is analogous to the bifurcation. Before the new branching becomes clear, there seems to be a considerable chaos; after it becomes clear, there seems to be more complex order.

Another way to think about transition and bifurcation is to think about before-having-a-first-baby to postpartum family development. In this example, in the "before" state, life seems to have a stable set of family relations configurations. Then, fairly quickly, something happens, and after a period of greater disorder, several new configurations within the new three-person family branch off on their own tracks. Earlier we had variations on a parent–parent relational theme; later we have three possible centers of relations (the original one and Parent #1 to child and Parent #2 to child). In the example of the birth of a first child, we know what the proximate cause was that got the system to transform. In some bifurcating systems the push to transformation is not so well known.

IMPLICATIONS

What might such a theory as chaos imply about reality? First, it suggests that there is more than one sort of disorder. Useful, chaotic disorder provides fresh options and room to correct for past errors; useless disorder provides nothing that seems meaningful, now or later. For example, Smith and Thelan (1993) describe in chaotic-system terms the very young child's learning to walk. Surprisingly, that learning is not a simple practice of muscle movements of a predetermined type. Instead, the child randomly (or so it seems) tries out various movements somewhat associated with walking, finally settling on the best set which allows for the most efficient walking behavior to occur. In other words, the child uses randomness in service to creation of an individualized optimal pattern for a skill which had been encoded in the human behavioral repertoire and was now emergent.

Second, chaos theory suggests and implies the immense importance of each element in the system for the final outcome of the system as well as for the individual. Remember, a perturbation caused by one butterfly's wing can alter the weather pattern, besides allowing the butterfly to fly. And in our own personal histories, we all remember those small chance remarks or experiences that led to major life changes. Chaos principles help validate our phenomenological experience.

Third, chaos theory suggests the importance of openness to innovation to provide natural sorts of corrective devices for complex events, especially those events in which outcomes and goals are not totally clear to us. In that kind of event a good process is our only safeguard against a manipulation that could cause unimagined damage when it has unforeseen consequences for a dynamical system. For example, we now understand the dangers we face by severely limiting the types of food crops we cultivate. Hundreds of variations on any given food crop species have been lost when we selected for the single species with the high yield. But in the event that a disease attacks that one species (as in the famous Irish potato famine of the last century) we would have lost the chance to recover because our process of dealing with multiple types of plant species was flawed.

What might chaos theory imply for lifespan cognitive development? We might begin to conceptualize lifespan cognitive development as a potentially chaotic system. If we do so, we would not expect to find many simple deterministic relationships. We would expect that some deterministic basic elements might be found, but that they will likely be the underlying, hidden order beneath the apparent disorder.

The system of lifespan cognitive development may be a structurally unstable system, subject to the large effects of tiny perturbations. As Cavanaugh and McGuire (1994) note, however, the whole idea in developmental research is to show how states change over time in a variety of individualized ways. Using chaos concepts, we can predict types of relationships during periods of relative stability in the lifespan and can predict ranges of variability and points of transition to unstable structures. This may not satisfy our desires to predict deterministically from moment to moment, but it may be a more realistic goal and a prime opportunity to study complex individual differences.

Predicting factors that lead to bifurcations of systems, for example, predictions about the events that trigger a bifurcation between formal and postformal logical thought in a person, can be made and tested empirically. The new center of events in that case, that is, postformal reasoning as the advanced thinking process of an adult, might then be described as a strange attractor.

Cavanaugh and McGuire (1994) suggest that chaos theory can help us frame and answer several questions about adult cognitive development. It would offer insights as to why there are just a few qualitatively unique levels of thinking. It could help explain why cognitive development shows a few "spurts" at certain times but smooth progression most of the time. It could address why cognitive flexibility (i.e., moving easily among attractors so as to solve problems creatively) is so hard to maintain. It could show how modes of thinking develop. And it could resolve the persistent question of why cognitive training usually does not generalize.

Self-Organizing Systems

Self-organizing systems carry the ideas of chaotic nonlinear systems one step further, by examining what happens when such systems reach conditions that are very far from their state of equilibrium. At that point, systems reorganize themselves in unpredictable ways that are sometimes so dramatic (even if they are just computer models) that the term "artificial life" has been used to describe them (Waldrop, 1992).

The Santa Fe Institute was created to explore phenomena related to self-organizing systems and has become a kind of Mecca for complexity theorists. Interested readers may wish to explore this field in several books, including those by Goldstein (1994) (on organizational change), Kauffman (1993) (on evolution), Kelly (1994), Maturana and Varela (1980) (on adaptive cognition), Nicholis and Prigogene (1989), and Waldrop (1992).

KEY CONCEPTS

We tend to think of collective behavior as simply the accumulation of individual behavior, but it is more than that. Collective behavior tends to be nonlinear and tends toward self-organization. One molecule or one person (ignoring for the moment that persons are systems) may respond in a particular way to being pushed past its limits, while a collection of those molecules or persons will respond very differently and somewhat unpredictably. Self-organizing systems studies work with the unique properties of such collectives. Self-organization has the following features when it occurs, according to Goldstein (1994): system structure is radically reorganized; novel patterns emerge; random events are amplified and utilized; and a new coordination of parts is attained. These changes are not imposed on the system but emerge from it. Collective systems do not simply resist change or face destruction, but have the potential to ride the change to create a different organization within. The changes are self-orchestrated as this system reconfigures its own resources in the face of a far-from-equilibrium challenge.

Goldstein (1994) describes some characteristics of self-organization: a spontaneous and radical reorganizing occurs; equilibrium-seeking tendencies are interrupted; the system utilizes the disorganization as a chance for change within some limits; and unpredictable outcomes occur which leave the system more optimally organized.

Complexity theory goes beyond qualitative descriptions of the kind of systems it deals with, namely, complex *adaptive* systems, by making complexity a quantity that is measurable. Complex systems also have similar qualities in whatever context they occur.

IMPLICATIONS

The implications of this theory are simply too vast to be outlined yet. Imagine a unified theory of adaptive system change being applied to everything and this will give the scope of possibilities. Few topics are off limits. Possibilities include prediction of developmental trends in adulthood and aging as multiple adaptive systems interact over time. It is not difficult to see the self-organizing qualities of intimate interactive systems.

Complex Thought and Emotionally Experienced Close Relationships

A S WE EXPLORE THE CONNECTION BETWEEN COGNITION AND relationship satisfaction, we need to examine *where, exactly, at what point,* cognition might intersect with relationships. A little more specifically, how does complex problem-solving ability affect emotionally salient (or "felt") connections and relationships? We need a general perspective before moving on to study any specific processes. To approach these questions more effectively we need to begin to develop a theory of complex thought and emotionally experienced (or "felt") relationships.

Felt connections are emotionally experienced relationships. What relation do felt connections—emotionally experienced connections among aspects of the self, between self and another, and between self and some transcendent value, belief, or meaning—have to do with complex postformal cognition?

Cognitive development at every point in the lifespan can be considered an *adaptive* transformation of the self, a dance of transformation that demands constant movement and balance. The mechanisms of assimilation and accommodation are used to modify cognition so that the adult organism—in this case, a person—survives and even flourishes in a given environment. A consistent sense of self is maintained in a meaningful life experience that includes emotional connections with intimate others.

The features of cognition that are uniquely adaptive in adulthood include organic integration of "inside" (the self and its parts) and "outside" (other persons) and "transcendent" (something or someone larger than the self that gives life meaning) knowledge structures. This requires a self-referential complex "new physics" (Sinnott, 1989a, 1993a, 1994a, 2004b) type of logic—in my terms, complex postformal thought. A person develops such an epistemological reasoning through challenges from interactions with emotionally important others who see the world and that person differently. Adult reasoning is refined further to become even more adaptive, by means of struggles to know and integrate the often contradictory sides of the personality/self, and to know and integrate felt connections with some transcendent that is larger than the self. Cognition is an *adaptive* developmental dance.

Cognition as an Adaptive Developmental Dance

One of the most important features of development and learning is that *adaptation* of the organism is a paramount goal that serves both organism and environment. Sometimes, reading lifespan development research and theory, we get the feeling that the human is still the center of the psychological and biological universe. We get the impression that psychological processes just *are,* for their own sakes, without reference to their effectiveness at keeping us alive and thriving.

Mechanisms for adaptive cognitive development and processing allow for a gradual good fit between the organism and the environment. The processes rest on the well-known activities of assimilation and accommodation. In *assimilation,* already-present knowing schemata take in new information in a way that fits the pattern they already possess. If that pattern proves inadequate to the occasion, *accommodation* begins to reshape the schemata. The final product is a set of schemata that better fit the environment the person wishes to know.

Similar sorts of mechanisms allow development of more complex levels of cognition that fit the more complex situation of the growing child and adult. When enough discrete elements of information are learned with small modifications in schemata, a rich enough matrix may permit a shift to a new level of complexity of cognition, driven, still, by its potential power to aid adaptation. The more complex cognitive level may be the most adaptive way to process some epistemological tasks; a simpler level may be the most adaptive way to process others. Examples of this will appear later. Again, the most important word in this process is *adaptive*.

But what do adults, in contrast to children and adolescents, need to adapt *to*? Here I am talking about adults in general to simplify our discussion. There are a few demands that have an impact on adults in general and that demand some adaptation in our epistemology, that is, in how we know reality.

The first demand is that, with the passage of life time, we need to form close relationships with others (recall Erikson's intimacy and generativity; Erikson, 1982). For these relationships to work, for some of the time at least, we need to "know" similar realities together. For example, is our marriage healthy or not? Are we good friends? Sometimes we need to arrive at the same judgment of truth or quality along with someone important to us. Are we being treated fairly in our workplace? Is this "quality" work? Is it good for our son to go to war?

The second demand is that we need to keep a consistent sense of self while also personally changing and being challenged by contradictions over time. For example, can I be a "good" person if I sometimes do "bad" things? How can I reconcile my sense of self as independent and strong with the facts of my personal aging and my varied behavior from relationship to relationship and from subculture to subculture? How can I make an integrated story of my life and my "self" (recall Erikson's "integrity") when my life has had so many turns and twists? As McAdams describes in detail in his 2013 article, "The Psychological Self as Actor, Agent, and Author," the psychological self is a complex construction of the subjective "I" and the constructed "me" over the lifetime. And it does have a cognitive component, of greater or lesser complexity.

The third demand is that, if, as many adults do, I give importance to some spiritual meaning or transcendent value for life and death, I need to reconcile my knowing existence as everyday, finite, and material with my knowing existence as somehow larger, spiritual, and transcendent. Notice that the demand for knowing the "truth" of these realities cannot be met very adaptively simply by picking one pole or the other of the apparent dichotomies. A reasoning is required that says "yes" to both, that both are "true."

In addition to examining demands to see what adults must adapt to, I might examine the complex ways of knowing of my many adaptive older relatives, or the ways of knowing of thinkers such as Einstein. When I do this I also see the need for theorists to develop a description of uniquely adult adaptive cognitive complexity. Einstein's wonderful descriptions of relativity, the knowledge of the universe delivered by the "new physics," and the wise pronouncements of my relatives all demand an additional epistemology to account for adult knowledge of a non-egocentric but self-referential truth *in addition to* a scientific truth. A self-referential truth, defined in terms of physics, is that light is both a wave and a particle simultaneously, and the scientist must *choose* which way to regard it, thereby (partially) creating the "truth" of the situation.

A "Dancing Self" Metaphor and Intimate Relationships

The metaphor of self-transformation as a dance is important to this discussion. Picture a village circle dance, a traditional folk dance. These folk dances often are said to represent the dance of life (or some part of it) in which we all participate. In any circle dance, each of us, in our uniqueness, is important to the dance. Without us, in fact, there would be no dance; traditional village dances are participatory activities, not paid performances.

In order for the dance to take place, three kinds of relational skills have to be mastered and integrated. The relational skills are analogous to felt connections, discussed later in the chapter; the integration is analogous to postformal cognitive operations, also discussed later. First, each of us has to have some balance within the self to move smoothly through the steps of the dance; otherwise we end up stepping on our own feet. Second, each of us has to interact skillfully and flexibly with other dancers in the circle, or we might crash into each other and fall down. Third, each of us needs to remain connected with the overall purpose of the dance, attuned to the kind of dance this is today, or the circle dance will lose any meaningful pattern. And all these activities must be integrated.

We are each a part of this communal dance activity, but at no time does a self, one of the dancers, disappear. Paradoxically, the more a self learns to be balanced and interwoven and interconnected, the more that single self becomes important to the creation of the dance, perhaps even leading other dancers.

Regulation of Stimulation Overload

At each stage of life, the organism is confronted with sometimes overwhelming stimulation and multiple emotional and intellectual demands that must be regulated in service to survival. Any adult is faced with demands for food, drink, and bonds with others, and also is faced with some additional stage-specific demands. The new ones are generated by the broader social identity usually created in adulthood. Any adult with a full life can describe how over-whelming these may be. Some sets of demands come from family (children and older parents), community, social institutions, and work; others come from the sheer number of tasks to perform, bills to pay, information to assimilate. Sometimes it all feels like too much.

The formal reasoning system for resolving any one of these relationship-related tasks may not be logically compatible with that for resolving another. Generating more systems may help, since this productivity may provide more adequate answers to life's dilemmas. But the ante has been raised by life; there are too many contradic-tory demand and information systems. At this point of overload the reasoning of postformal operations may help solve the ill-structured problems of adult life that involve relationships with others. In a best-case scenario, the cognitive demands could lead to a higher-level *restructuring* and *development* of logical abilities through which the problem is more easily solved, allowing close relationships to stay satisfying.

The Overloaded Self

A situation of overload exists when the knower cannot effectively process the amount of information that presents itself. The self who processes this amount is in danger of becoming fragmented. Although postformal thought gives the knower more to think about, thereby potentially *causing* overload, postformal thought is a powerful tool for *reducing* overload adaptively, by organizing information and feelings.

Of course, there are *mal*adaptive and *non*creative ways to reduce overload. For example, overloaded adults may limit their cognitive stimulation by limiting their experience to those situations where only one formal reasoning system, or only concrete operational logic, needs to be considered. In other words, they might rigidly interpret all cognitive events through the filter of their limited belief system about any relationship. In the realm of personality, such a person might deny various aspects of the self because there are no cognitive resources available to deal with the complexity.

The overload dilemma might be resolved more creatively and adaptively, though, through postformal thought. These complex operations provide an advantage over formal operations by permitting consolidation across those conflicting systems of logical realities so that more complex meaning and interactions might be available to the thinker. Consensus understandings and maximal use of large amounts of information would be possible. Sides of the self could be acknowledged and synthesized.

Maturity probably brings understanding and acceptance of the necessary subjectivity of knowledge (one of the characteristics of postformal thought), whether it is about people or events or objects. This acceptance makes it easier to tolerate others' beliefs and ways of life. If the knower has postformal thought, he or she looks with an empathic eye, rather than with annoyance, on the younger family member's painful struggles to make the truth of the world or people into absolute, unchanging truth. The knower can sympathize with less skilled individuals' defense of what they hope is the "right" way of doing something; the knower remembers when he or she was formal operational and felt the same way. Postformal thought can maximize the availability of information while minimizing relational and social conflict.

Coping with Overstimulation

If postformal thought is not available, various means of coping with overstimulation and overload might be used in close relationships.

Sometimes these creative coping strategies are available at the cost of adaptivity. Since adult coping is so often found in the realm of interpersonal cognition, let's look at examples of coping strategies in that domain. For example, consider a middle-aged adult with a family, a career, civic responsibilities, and a social life. This person is faced with endless demands to "fit" the data of this social world by choosing a viable formal-operational system for interacting with each partner, family member, or friend. If this adult makes these choices and solves these interpersonal problems, it will not happen by means of formal operations alone. Postformal operations will provide the best possible match, because postformal creative processes will provide the largest number of inclusive, real-life problem-solving possibilities for this ill-structured "fuzzy set" problem of felt relationships.

Following are some possible *un*creative, *non*-postformal solutions to overload in interpersonal midlife contexts.

1. The adult might reduce stimulation by limiting the self and retreating cognitively, perceiving all interpersonal relations at a lower level of cognitive or emotional complexity. Instead of "receiving" the behavior of others as the others have "sent" it, or trying to receive it at a higher and more integrated level, the adult might *interpret the behavior at a lower level*, that is, in a more simplistic way. For example, instead of trying to understand the relations that are possible with a certain individual, the adult may resort to dealing with him or her only as a member of a racial group, because this limit lets him or her preserve the self.

2. The adult might reduce overload by *developing a rigid social identity* that permits only certain messages to be received. If, in such a case, the adult has a self-definition capable of only certain relations with others, other relational stimuli are ignored. All problems are oversimplified.

3. The adult can reduce overload by *focusing on only selected goals or interests*, again limiting the self. The effect of this tactic is similar to the effect of the second tactic. All levels of complexity are available to be used in analyzing an event, but the individual limits the types of content considered.

In contrast, following are some possible creative, adaptive, solutions to overload and "self" preservation that make use of postformal cognition in these ill-structured relationship problems.

1. The adult might reduce overload by understanding the *many* possible reasoning structures that can underlie a perceived interaction. The is an adaptive strategy that can only come from experience and familiarity with many types of systems and possession of postformal thought, which holds all logics as possible simultaneously. If the receiver can *match reception (from the complex self) to the encoded level of the transmitted message*, conflict can be reduced. The key to this ability is to access a good system of transformations to relate the sets of coordinates using postformal operations.

2. The adult might reduce stimulus overload by making a *more efficient total integration*, again using the self as a *complex* filter. Developing the integrative skill is an adaptive solution to overload. It makes use of complex theorizing that is based on experience. No content or complexity is lost when this technique is used. The mapping surface is so large and the topography so varied that most messages fit in somewhere, through use of postformal thought. In the storage closet of the mind, overload clutter that has an interpretive place is no longer really "overload." Defined in relation to the fuller self, it has a meaningful place.

Adult Cognitive Development: Cognition with Felt Connection

What relation does felt connection—connection among aspects of the self, between self and another, and between self and a Transcendent—have to complex postformal cognition and learning? *Felt connection* can be defined as conscious awareness of relatedness to another with an emotional-attachment component. Adult cognitive development and the development of complex *felt* connection are motivated by *each other* and ultimately influence each other.

That interrelationship is described in a new theory (Sinnott, 2005, 2006; Sinnott & Berlanstein, 2006), summarized in Figure 1.

Let's look at each part of the figure and enlarge upon the complex ideas we find there. Seven aspects of ideas in the figure are outlined

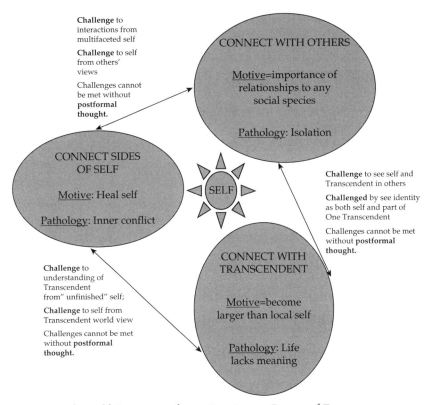

FIGURE 1 The Self Experienced as a Consistent Center of Events: Challenges from Multiple Relationships Coordinated by Complex Cognition.

in the next sections. These aspects are based on research and earlier theoretical work on felt connection. Suggestions for future research can be found in Sinnott and Berlanstein (2006). This aspect of the theory is newer and so cannot yet enjoy as much empirical support as other aspects of postformal theory.

Three Types of Feeling Connected

The first part of Figure 1 to notice is that there are three types of feeling connected. These three elements are labeled "connect the sides of the self," "connect with others," and "connect with the Transcendent." *Connecting the sides of the self* involves being in touch with and relating to the various aspects of our personalities, including disowned parts like the Shadow (Jung, 1930/1971). How we connect the sides of ourselves (and the *existence* of "sides" of the self) partly depends on early relationships in the family of origin. *Connecting with others* involves interactions between or among persons, the conscious or unconscious interpersonal relationship pattern we exhibit today. *Connecting with the Transcendent* involves having an ongoing relationship with something or someone that is larger than the individual self, for example, The Great Spirit, the Universe, or God.

Three Dynamic Processes

In Figure 1 each of these three types of feeling connected is united with the other two by lines and arrows going in both directions, indicating that each of the three elements influences and is influenced by the others in a circular fashion. Therefore, there are *three dynamic processes*, the dynamics of which we can discuss and study. The first process is the dynamic interplay between "connecting the sides of the self" and "connecting with others." The second process is the dynamic interplay between "connecting with others" and "connecting with the Transcendent." The third process is the dynamic interplay between "connecting with the Transcendent" and "connecting the sides of the self." Interventions and applications, described later, may make use of one or more of these three dynamic processes.

Challenges to the Self/Identity as We Relate to Intimates

As humans we paradoxically desire both continuity and change, close connection and freedom. The dynamic interaction processes (those two arrows uniting any two elements in Figure 1) also are described in terms of the *challenges* to the self, challenges posed by the simultaneous experience of any two types of connected feelings. The two types of connected feelings may not agree with each other.

When I speak of "self" here, I refer to a dynamic, changing center of events with which a person identifies at a human, ego level, even as it may be constantly transforming. An adaptive characteristic of the human cognitive process is to form concepts and label them as distinct from other concepts. At the same time, the same human thinker might also understand that, on the level of physics or mysticism, this seemingly concrete thing, the self, is an illusion.

In the dynamic interaction between "connecting sides of the self" and "connecting with others" two challenges occur. The self that exists at any one time is called into question by experiencing the reality of others, and the manner in which one perceives and relates to others is transformed as more sides of the self are accepted.

In the dynamic interaction between "connecting with others" and "connecting with the Transcendent" two challenges occur. The manner in which we perceive and relate to others may be changed by our growing awareness of the Transcendent. And our connection with the Transcendent might change when challenged by the behavior of others close to us.

Motivation

The three sets of processes are also labeled with a *motivation* factor in Figure 1. That factor suggests *why* a person might want to do the difficult work of rising to the challenge of constructing and maintaining the self when new information emerges during the dynamic interactions. When the dynamic interaction process involves "connecting sides of the self" (coupled with some other element), motivation comes from the desire to be more complete or whole, to heal. When the dynamic interaction process involves the element of "connecting with others" (coupled with some other element), motivation comes from our desires to maintain and improve ties with people important to us. When the dynamic interaction process involves "connecting with the Transcendent" (coupled with some other element), motivation comes from the desire to increase our intimate connection with something spiritual, something larger than our local selves. Motivations can be both practical and existential.

Pathology

There can be a failure to feel connected within any single one of the three types of felt connections mentioned above: within the self, between the self and other persons, and with the Transcendent. These particular failures are labeled *pathology* in Figure 1. They have implications for identity and emotional wellbeing.

First, if there are failures in the development of the felt connections within the self, the person might experience inner conflicts, surprisingly conflicted or self-sabotaging decisions, and a feeling of fragility. The person tends to lose the self upon interacting with others. The person rigidly judges to be "bad" those persons who seem to represent the sides of the self that have not been accepted and integrated. Welwood (1996) discusses this form of projection, especially in the context of relationships.

Failure to establish felt connections with others might lead to different problems. For example, the person might feel isolated or abandoned, as if no one can understand him or her. Intimacy and generativity (Erikson, 1982) might not be possible, then, for that person.

Failure to establish connections with something or someone larger than the self, that is, with some transcendent meaning for life, may carry yet another set of problems. There may be an existential crisis. The person may be driven by anxiety about death, or may find life tragic and meaningless. For this person there is nothing that gives a larger platform from which to view current problems or setbacks.

These failures to feel intensely connected, and the resulting difficulties, leave the person with sadness and a yearning to reweave the web of life, to feel connected, to take part in the dance of life in some more coherent way. But we need those three things mentioned earlier to participate in a healthy way in our modern version of village circle dances. We need to feel mastery of many steps (connection within the self), to feel connected to other dancers in the circle (interpersonal connection), and to be in connection with the overall pattern the dance represents (connection with the Transpersonal or Transcendent). We need to feel the three types of connection or relationship.

Complex Postformal Thought and Felt Connection

Figure 1 also refers to *postformal thought* in relation to each challenge. To successfully integrate the types of connections and their sometimes disparate or conflicting ideas, yet preserve a concept of a self that is whole, postformal complex cognitive operations must be used (Sinnott, 1998b). The conflicting ideas, and the person's high motivation to work out the conflict, provide an occasion for the initial and continuing learning of this complex thinking ability. Possession of this thinking ability provides the means for more easily handling the challenge of conflicting relational structures.

However, a person may suffer from what might be called a *cognitive pathology*. Failure to develop complex postformal cognitive representations and some integration of the reality of the several types of felt connections, for whatever reason, leaves the self in a fragmented and conflicted state with few conscious cognitive tools to become whole. The person in such a state may never consciously conceptualize and grasp a way to be able to live with multiple strongly felt connections. Learning is needed. Some examples may clarify this point.

On a cognitive level it may seem impossible to such a person to integrate his or her connections with many other persons of all different types into a unified self that feels whole or connected inside. It will seem like either the whole, integrated self or the deep connections with other persons will have to be sacrificed. The problem is that the person cannot conceive of a way of connecting with others without losing the self, a very unsatisfactory "borderline" life outcome. Learning the integration can only occur with the learning and use of postformal complex thought.

In a second example of a cognitive failure, the person without complex cognitive representations may be faced with integrating felt connection with others and a felt connection to the Transcendent. The person may conceive of no alternatives but to give up a spiritual search (connection with the Transcendent) in favor of keeping connections with loved ones, or to break connections with the loved ones in order to continue a spiritual search. Again, the person's "solution" leads to a less than satisfactory adult development outcome due to (unnecessary) either/or choices and loss of felt connection of some type. Only a postformal cognitive representation of self would integrate both aspects of felt connection. Learning can foster this (Sinnott, 1998b).

A final example might add additional clarity. The person who cannot cognitively represent the complex process of integrating two types of felt connection may have a third type of problem: That person may not be able to conceive of knowing and accepting the multiple sides of the self (some sides of self considered "good," some considered "less than good") *and* feeling (guiltlessly) connected with an angry God figure. A resolution could only occur if one set of felt connections is sacrificed (e.g., surrender of self to the Divine Will or give up religion or a spiritual life). Again, the *non*-resolution, based on the inability to conceptualize in postformal terms at a more complex level, closes off life options for growth and for feeling connected and whole in multiple ways simultaneously.

Learning and Development

Finally, how do *learning and development* intersect in the model represented in Figure 1? We have already touched upon these relations. The ideas of assimilation and accommodation are helpful in understanding the intersection of concepts. In Figure 1, when a challenge occurs, the individual receiving new information first tries to assimilate the new information into the cognitive concepts he or she already holds. Those current concepts fit the person's current developmental level. If there is a challenge, however, the new information will not fit the old concepts and ways of being in the world. If the individual who is challenged does not ignore that new information but accommodates to it, learning takes place. For a longer discussion of learning and development in adults from this perspective, see Sinnott (1994b, 1998b). At some point a new developmental level may result from a combination of organic growth and the learning of newly acquired information.

From the preceding discussion we see how a person *could* come to have a coherent way of thinking about and working with relations that exist in all three areas noted in Figure 1: within the self (based on early experience), interpersonal relations, or relationship with the Transcendent. As a person tries to balance or be *cognitively consistent* about close connections in all these areas of relationship, similarity in the existential story of the relationships will be sought because it would make thinking about them easier. If, for example, parts of me cannot be trusted, *and* others cannot be trusted, *and* God cannot be trusted, my thinking about life is simplified in one coherent pattern of distrust.

Cognitive Prerequisites for Relationship Growth and Their Outcomes

Some learning must take place before a person can use complex postformal thought in close relationships. A person needs to have some access to logical thought, and needs to have some experience with close relationships with all their necessary complexity. That person needs to have encountered and struggled with the type of problem-solving that deals with what are termed "ill-structured" problems in which the goal and parameters of the problem are somewhat unclear. Luckily, life provides a generous supply of those. And, of course, the person needs to have a certain amount of memory, attention, and intelligence to work with.

Gradually, these problem-solving processes are applied to emotionally intense, felt connections. For example, instead of seeing only one possible way to structure a relationship, the person sees that we create the set of "givens" that we use as the basis of the relationship. The person gradually starts to learn that the intimate partner can never absolutely be "known," since "knowing" is always, to some degree, a construction of truth. The person gradually begins to see that relationships are always a *process*, rather than, for example, a role, and cannot be described in a stable way until they end. These are just a few examples of what must be understood before cognition of interpersonal relationships becomes complex in nature.

Several abilities are needed before people can completely access postformal thought in understanding relationships (or in understanding anything else) on a deeper level. First, they must be able to access a "scientific" formal reasoning (i.e., have access to "formal" operational logic). Then they must start to acquire the ability to use various thinking operations (noted earlier) that ultimately make up postformal thought. There must be acceptance of the potential validity of more than one way to see a given event (make a priori choice of a belief system among many belief systems about the event). They need to understand that a given act can lead to various outcomes in differing contexts (multiple solutions) and that, conversely, an outcome might have several causes (multi-causality) and goals. They need to begin understanding that contradiction, subjectivity, and choice are inherent even in "logical" and "objective" events that are frequently paradoxical; therefore, one must choose the limits of the problem and solution by using problem definition and pragmatism. Finally, they must realize that sometimes the "best" solution to a problem is a good process-to-solution.

Relationship behavior looks different when people only have access to *formal* reasoning in thinking about relationships compared with when they have access to *postformal* reasoning as well. Here are some comparisons:

When people think formally, they are more likely to believe there is only a *single* way that an intimate relationship can possibly be structured to make it work; when they can think postformally they are more likely to believe that their intimate relationship is fine if it is within their chosen set of "givens" about relationships.

When they think formally, the relationship seems to be a concrete thing out there in reality; when postformal thought is possible they are more likely to believe that their relationship is constantly being co-created by them.

When they think formally, the relationship seems to involve only "us" right now; when postformal thought is possible, the relationship is seen to encompass multiple causes and contexts, and complex views of "us."

When they think formally they are more sure that the relationship has one and only one reality, and each partner should be able to see that reality IF they are operating in good faith; from a postformal perspective partners see that a relationship is always "in process," never stable, until it ends.

Formal reasoning suggests that each partner can really know the essence of the other partner; postformal reasoning suggests that by "knowing you" I am always partially subjectively creating the reality of you, that the "essence" of the other is fleeting.

The formal partner is likely to believe that playing the right relationship *role* is more important than process; the postformal thinker is likely to believe that the process of relating is much more important than the roles we play within one.

Felt connection—emotionally charged connection—with others intersects with thinking in these complex ways.

Social, Cultural, and Historical Factors Relate to Cognitive Aspects of Intimate Relationships

THIS CHAPTER HIGHLIGHTS SOME VERY IMPORTANT AND sometimes very recently studied social, cultural, and historical factors, all of which interface with cognitive aspects of intimate relationships.

Understanding relationships is so difficult under the best of circumstances that it is not surprising that we turn away from an even bigger picture, that of the social forces within which those human interactions are nested. When we psychologists study the cognitive aspects of these relationships, we may be especially tempted to focus on the individual who does that thinking, rather than on variables surrounding that individual thinker.

In this chapter I hope to call attention to just a few of the recent approaches that might prove useful in our thinking about these broader variables and relationships. We want to think about many new questions such broader explorations raise, for example:

How does the complex understanding of relationship satisfaction affect the creation and style of broader social bonds, and visa-versa?

How do culture and the complex understanding of intimate relationships connect with or mutually influence each other?

How does the historical period in which we live relate to our complex understanding of intimate relationships?

How does our way of conceptualizing multi-person, or political, or societal relationships in the larger world relate to our way of conceptualizing personal intimate relationships?

Numerous recent books have examined the evolving patterns of societies over historical time. Many changes during those evolutions are linked to specific styles of conceptualizing relationships, the world, the human adventure, and the individual's role in all these. A multitude of social, historical, and cultural changes and differences can be linked to understanding of relationships using general systems theory processes and processes common to self-constructing living systems. Let's take a look at just a few of these recent "big picture" theoretical explorations, to see how they relate to the topic of this book, cognitive aspects of intimate relationships. They may offer additional suggestions for research.

As we explore these connections, be aware that thinking and problem-solving in complex cognitive ways, as in postformal thought, form the underpinning of both adaptive relationships and adaptive social and cultural processes. Thinking postformally, whether the thinking is about intimate relationships, or morality and social processes, or the varied processes of world religions, it is a cognitive process that enables the balance of differing logics and points of view. This process bridges across differences to allow functioning in complex situations having heightened motivation or emotion.

Historical Changes and Cognitive Aspects of Intimate Relationships

Our first stop in this more inclusive journey is a book very closely connected to spouse and partner relationships, Stephanie Coontz's influential *Marriage, a History: From Obedience to Intimacy, or How Love Conquered Marriage* (2005). Coontz makes the compelling argument that the historical entity that is marriage-like has been conceptualized in many different ways over historical time in the West, based on the pressures and needs of the times. This evolution changed what partners conceptualized (the cognitive element) as a "satisfying" or "thriving" relationship.

For most of Western history marriage was *not* thought of as being about love or mutual satisfaction or emotional and friendship needs. These would have been considered irrational and no basis on which to build a family or, by extension, a society. Rather, marriage was conceptualized as a connection based on social roles, property exchange, and the need for population. In this context "satisfaction" and "thriving" meant that partners were playing their roles well, bringing property or wealth to their union and their extended families, and having many offspring. Partners having done these things, cognitive construct-based demands of the experience (as constructed by society) were fulfilled, and cultural concepts and personal concepts were in agreement.

However, in more recent times, the union of partners to serve property and wealth became less life-saving for individuals who could more easily "go it alone." There also was no longer a need for so many children in the West since more survived to adulthood and were not as economically important in an industrial economy. Personally fulfilling emotional relationships, for both men and women, were expected in the new economic reality of the nineteenth and later centuries. At that point partnerships became both more emotionally fulfilling and more fragile, as the feelings of fulfillment could come and go and the "degree of those feelings" defined (the cognitive part again) the nature of "satisfying" and "thriving" relationships. By definition, at that point in history, intimate relationships were constructed as less stable, since feelings come and go.

If the concept of marriage as a committed role and the concept of marriage as a reflection of personal feelings conflict in a relational situation, these formal reasoning analyses of the situation could lead to personal conflict and dissatisfaction. If such a situation is conceptualized through a postformal lens, however, there is a possibility of satisfactory resolution.

Note the link among three things: the needs of an historical epoch, the definition of "satisfying relationship," and the impact of relationship changes for social structures large and small. Although Coontz's book focuses on marriage, we can see that the same dynamic would apply to other intimate relationships, such as parent–child or friendship or sibling relationships. If the purpose is *conceived of* as utilitarian or role-related, the form of the interactions and the impact on society, culture, and history suits that definition. Then if social changes happen, and the concept of the interactional expectations correspondingly changes, the press for yet another changing form of intimate relationships becomes stronger.

Therefore, this is a circular phenomenon: change in concepts of social needs leads to change in concepts of intimate relationships, and that, in turn, leads to changes in next-generation concepts of the larger society and future social needs. We can theorize about the research questions that should be asked in regard to cognitive factors, conceptualization of relationships, and concepts of ideal historical or societal relationships. See Figure 2 for a description of the circular evolving relationship between cognitive constructions of intimate relationships and cognitive constructions of cultural, social, and historical relationships.

The Ascendance of Empathic Cultures and Cognitive Aspects of Intimate Relationships

Let's look at another sweeping take on relationships in history, society, and culture and see where there may be a connection between complex cognitive constructions of relationships and larger social and historical forces. Jeremy Rifkin's *The Empathic Civilization* (2009) examines a new view of human nature, namely, the increasing development of empathy in human culture and its consequences for communication, relationships, and cultures. These consequences can be both personal and general.

If human beings are not by nature aggressive, materialistic, utilitarian, and self-interested, but rather are now more empathic, how does this shape our close relationships and our fate as a species? Where is the cognitive/relationship satisfaction element here?

For one thing, greater evolving empathic awareness is a change in conceptualization of the "other." In deeper empathy, what is the

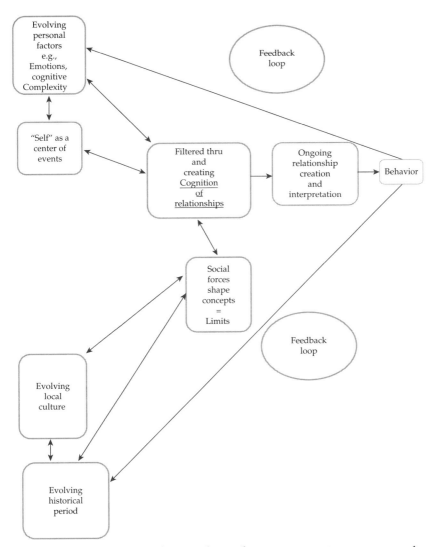

FIGURE 2 The Circular Evolving Relationship: Cognitive Constructions of Intimate Relationships and Cognitive Constructions of Cultural, Social, and Historical Relationships Co-Construct Each Other Over Time. Notes: Figure 2 represents a self-constructing living system, or, on a finer level of analysis, several self-constructing living systems. It also represents the order underlying apparent chaos of close relationships. Figure 2 assumes an individual "self" that is defined as a center of events, moving over time. Finally, Figure 2 assumes that new information obtained through the feedback loops *can* be assimilated by the individual, by the local culture, and by the larger historical context, leading to ongoing development.

concept of "me" and what is the concept of "us-in-relationship"? Can our intimate relationship feel "satisfying" if we cannot understand the other's concept of "us"?

Also, note the historical element. For example, people who lived in aboriginal hunting and gathering cultures might have thought differently about relationships; they did not express ideas about relationships in written words. Written language demands that one think as if she or he is the other; the more I translate my thoughts to express them to another, the more I can conceptualize myself as a unique self, separate from the other. What effect might that have on the cognition of relationships and the style of the necessary problem-solving when concepts differ?

Jumping to the psychological consciousness of later times, how can the growing awareness of my thoughts lead to the desire for feeling understood by a significant other? Does that change what I want from a satisfying close relationship? What happens, then, for example, to the more rigid relational roles inherited from an earlier theological consciousness or to the highly rational societal values and roles of the Enlightenment period? It is easy to see many potential research questions about the circular relationships among the variables of history, culture, empathic cognition, and relationship satisfaction. Again, see Figure 2 for a description of the circular evolving relationship between cognitive constructions of cultural, social, and historical relationships and cognitive constructions of intimate relationships and the self.

Historical Decline of Violence and Cognitive Aspects of Intimate Relationships

This naturally leads us to examine Steven Pinker's 2011 book, *The Better Angels of Our Nature: Why Violence Has Declined*. Pinker documents the decline in violence worldwide over the centuries up to the present time. He suggests that the key to explaining the decline in violence is our understanding of the forces that promote violence (such as tribalism) and those forces that steer us away from violence. Under the influence of those forces that steer us *away* from violence, we increasingly control our impulses, empathize with others even when they appear different from us, bargain rather than plunder, turn from toxic ideologies, and use reason to reduce our tendencies to violence.

It does not seem surprising that, on the face of it, the techniques of reducing violence seem to rest on similar complex cognitions to the ones we use to make close relationships thrive. Can we predict a nation's level of violence by understanding the cognitive complexity of that nation's way of thinking about intimate relationships? Could the widespread use of complex postformal thought to reduce relational difficulties then also extend to an entire culture and be a predictor of its degree of violence? Again, see Figure 2 for a description of the circular evolving relationship between cognitive constructions of cultural, social, and historical relationships and cognitive constructions of intimate relationships.

Complex Understanding of Intimate Relationships and Success or Failure of Societies

A fourth stop on this journey of "big picture" ideas is a series of books on the success and failure of nations. First there is Diamond's *Guns, Germs, and Steel: The Fates of Human Societies* (1999), followed by his book *Collapse: How Societies Choose to Fail or Succeed* (2005). Diamond's argument in the first book is that gaps in power and technology among human societies originate in environmental differences that are amplified by positive feedback over time. In the second book he argues that societal collapses involve dysfunctional relationships between the environmental component, neighbors, and trade partners. One even broader analysis along these lines is *Why Nations Fail: The Origins of Power, Prosperity, and Poverty* (Acemoglu & Robinson, 2012). This book offers the argument that the difference between wealth and poverty, between health and sickness, between food and famine, among nations (that may be in close proximity to one another geographically and environmentally) is due to culturally created political and economic systems of relationships. Are members of that society empowered by inclusive institutional relationships? If they are, we see positive results for the society as a whole.

Some intriguing ideas are suggested by these three books on the success or failure of societies, ideas that have some concordance with the ideas about intimate relationships in this book. In each of these three books the underlying factor that separates the historical, societal, and cultural "survivors and those who thrive" from the historical, cultural, and societal "failures" is the conceptualization of the relationships between individuals and the earth, the state, and each other. Note that we once again see the power of conceptualization of relationships. How we *think* about these relationships, in complex or simple ways, matters.

We might fruitfully study how the cognitive complexity (or lack of it) of key important relationships, inherent in a culture and expressed in politics, economics, inclusion, and environmental behaviors, is related to this larger national success or failure. What would a cognitively complex postformal model of politics, economics, environment, and inclusion look like? Then, can creating a thriving complex intimate relationship with a significant other teach us processes of complex thinking that generalize to our larger national decisions and promote complex inclusiveness in *those* relationships? In turn, does living in a complex relationally inclusive society come full circle to foster complex, satisfying intimate relationships between individuals? Figure 2 would suggest this is so.

The Political Brain, Cognition, and Cognitive Aspects of Intimate Relationships

According to Drew Westen, writing in *The Political Brain* (2007), in politics reason and emotion collide and emotion seems to win. People vote first on the basis of their feelings toward parties and the parties' principles, then only secondarily on their feelings toward the candidates, and third (only if they still have not decided) on the policies of the candidates. Westen approaches the exploration of this complexity from the dual point of view of his roles as a scientist who studies emotions and personality and as a neuroscientist studying the brain's processing of political information. He also is a clinician who explores the nuances and meanings of what people say and do. He puts these sets of insights together to try to understand what happens in the brains of individuals as they try to assess political information.

Returning to the topic of the present book, how might complex cognition, intimate relationships, and behavior in the political brain intersect with one another? As we know, close relationships involve *both* feeling and thinking. Relationships are not simply the product of a dispassionate rational mind. While the study of *close relationships* seems to have been short on examinations of the *cognitive* aspects of those relationships, the study of *political behavior* seems to have been short on examinations the *emotional* aspects of those behaviors. Yet, both thinking and emotions are involved in all these types of relationships.

As discussed earlier, when we put emotion and cognition together to study intimate relationships, we can move in new directions and make behavior in relationships clearer, *and* potentially more productive and satisfying. What we learn from increasing the complexity of understanding relationships, considering *both* emotion and cognition, we can also apply to the understanding of political forces and decisions. Asking, "Who *are* we in close relationships and what kind of relationship do we want to co-create for ourselves?" is not so different from asking, "Who *are* we as Americans who differ in many ways and what kind of society do we want to co-create for ourselves?"

Can we learn to construct more complex political behavior, based on, perhaps, learning a more complex cognitive construction of close relationships? Can the acceptance of a *complex* day-to-day construction of political action help facilitate the growth of complexity in intimate personal relationships? Is this, too, a circular evolving relationship as shown in Figure 2?

Morality, the "Righteous Mind," and Cognitive Aspects of Intimate Relationships

The second to last overview stop on our journey exploring the "big picture" of relationship satisfaction is in the land of concepts of morality. Our guide here is Jonathan Haidt, in his 2012 book, *The Righteous Mind: Why Good People Are Divided by Politics and Religion*. Righteousness, he notes is linked with, and sometimes defined by, being judgmental.

Haidt notes that intuitions precede reasoning, and that reason serves intuition, in the moral domain, at least. Examined globally, moral and ethical concerns may be about harm, fairness, liberty, loyalty, authority, and the sacred, and all of these are adaptive behaviors. The concerns may bind us together, but they may also blind us to the members of some other group that emphasizes different concerns. Each culture stresses some concerns of morality and turns a blind eye toward other concerns of morality. Also, our body states and emotional responses often override our conceptualizations, and in matters of morality and politics we tend to follow the group. According to Haidt, happiness comes from creating the right relationship between you, others, and something larger than the self.

Let's summarize some points Haidt makes in this book, points that relate to our understanding of similar relationship *forms* on a small and large scale.

> Morality is constructed by children, originally, on the basis of their experience of harm.
> Intuitions come first and strategic reasoning second.
> Intuitions can be shaped by reason, especially when they are shaped by interactions with others.
> In moral and political matters we are more often "groupish" than selfish.
> Society shapes relationships. People who grow up in Western educated, industrial, rich, democratic societies are more likely to perceive a world of separate objects rather than relationships.
> Emphasis varies on the relative importance of care, fairness, loyalty, sanctity, and authority.
> All these values evolved because they were adaptive.
> Genes and culture co-evolve.
> Human beings are conditioned "hive" creatures and morality and religion are, so to speak, "team sports."

In short, we view each other's morality and relationships from within our own moral matrix, one that is heavily laden with emotions and group feelings and relationship concepts. Our task is to make a cognitive *and* emotional bridge between these emotionally freighted views of the world. If we can do this bridging in our close relationships, aren't we more likely to do it in our political, social, and ethical lives? Conversely, if we are nurtured within a *social* matrix that values bridging logics, aren't we likely to learn to bridge logics in our *personal* intimate relationships? See Figure 2.

Spirituality and Cognitive Aspects of Intimate Relationships

Our last stop on our journey exploring connections between various "big picture" ideas and the topics of this book is the work of the well-known analyst of world religions, Huston Smith. Smith has explored, in great depth, the spiritual and religious systems of the world (see, for example, Smith, 1991, 1994, 2001, 2012). Smith concludes that there are four major "families" of world spiritual traditions that are known to us: South Asian (Hinduism and Buddhism), East Asian (Confucianism, Taoism, Zen Buddhism), Western (Judaism, Christianity, Islam), and Primal/Oral/Tribal. These families of spiritual traditions prefer different types of relationships among individuals, the physical and social world, and God. In other words, they make use of different logics in thinking about reality and our relational place in it.

As is obvious from even a casual observation of world history and our present times, the reasoning views of adherents of different religions themselves differ. We even see different concepts related to the religion of choice *within* a particular religion. The clash of logics, if it cannot be overcome in some way, is associated with religious wars and even clashes of civilizations. Adherents from the differing religious positions cannot "hear" each other's reasoning about the relationship between a person and the Transcendent, and react with profound emotion to the reasoning positions of the other. Much like angry couples, high emotionality and simplistic, black-and-white cognition drive two sets of believers away from each other. The worldviews of the two seem irreconcilable. There is a lack of complex postformal thinking.

Smith also writes of the adherents of "the perennial philosophy," mysticism, a more complex way of experiencing the spiritual life. What is most interesting to our discussion here is that every "family" of spiritual traditions has its mystics. And those mystics all understand a more complex spirituality, one with a complex reasoning that sounds postformal in its form. I have written about this in earlier publications (Sinnott, 1992, 1994a, 2000, 2001, 2002a b, 2003b, 2006, 2009b, 2010a, 2011). Whatever tradition they spring from, mystics "jump out" of the reasoning of their specific religious practice to consciously cognitively and emotionally choose to be in an overarching, bridging reasoning of Divine Love. This lets them bridge between seemingly contradictory religious systems to rest in a higher spiritual logic. Complex cognition about the relationship between the individual and God allows this overarching union of beliefs.

So how does this whole experience relate to the topic of the present book? We have argued that thinking about intimate relationships in a more cognitively complex way leads to beliefs and actions that make intimate relationships more satisfying over the long term. Two people can bridge differences and reach a new place of satisfaction with each other. The same seems true of religious traditions. If individuals are part of a religious tradition that uses complex thought to bridge differences of faith, they will be more likely to generalize these skills to their own relationships. If individuals practice complex thought–type interactions in their personal intimate relationships and find that satisfying, they will be more likely to generalize the ability to their religious and spiritual practices as well.

Once again consider the relationships expressed in Figure 2. Social, cultural, and historical factors set the stage for concepts that define intimate relationships and that are internalized by intimate partners. In turn, the forms of intimate relationships, in an ongoing way, help change the societies and cultures and so, ultimately, the history of a given period. This is an ongoing evolution.

Cognition and Fundamental Complex Relationship Skills

Theory-Limited Nonclinical Literature Related to Cognitive Factors in Intimate Relationships

H OW WE *THINK* ABOUT OUR RELATIONSHIPS INFLUENCES OUR *feelings* about those relationships; how we *feel* about our relationships influences what we *think* about them in the future. The more intense and intimate the relationship, the stronger this vicious or virtuous circle creates itself. In this way cognition (thought), feeling (emotion), social and historical factors, and personal history (development) are all key to relationship quality. Interpreted, conceptualized relationship quality can lead to a felt sense of satisfaction or dissatisfaction with the relationship itself and a judgment about the relationship's quality. We work to nurture relationships that we judge to be high in satisfaction. Therefore, our judgment, a cognitive process, can help them thrive or wane.

This chain of events, or, better still, *circle of events*, is usually described and studied in segments because of its complexity. One investigator might choose to focus on lifelong attachment style and relationship satisfaction, while another elects to focus on satisfaction ratings themselves, as a scale, and so forth. What actually is a circle, or a *complex self-constructing system*, erroneously appears to be a simpler linear cause–effect relationship because we forget it really is more complicated. Just as it is hard to honestly analyze in depth a wonderful piece of music by taking it apart note by note or passage by passage, it is hard to see the richness of satisfying, thriving relationships in ways that reduce the relationship to its smaller components.

It would be impossible to do justice to all of the excellent books on intimate relationships in a short chapter. For those readers who want more familiarity with a range of studies, a good introductory overview of the whole general circular process of close relationships, touching on all of its elements, can be found in a number of comprehensive reviews. These include those by Brown and Amatea (2000); Kelly and colleagues (1983); Miller, Perlman, and Brehm (2007); and Regan (2011).

Here, as elsewhere in this book, I cite important "classic" references as well as recent references. Both types are very useful. I also make use of both quantitative and qualitative types of investigations, since both of these approaches to knowledge-gathering have proved useful as well.

Some of my favorite books analyzing more specific topics in this larger intimate-relationships literature need to be mentioned here also. Carter and McGoldrick's (2005) special interest is the expanded family life cycle. Coontz (2005) examines the history of marriage as a concept. Goldberg (2010) discusses lesbian and gay parents and their children. Schwartz and Olds (2000) are most interested in the ebb and flow of lasting intimate relationships. Sternberg (1998) also writes about the course of love over time, nesting his approach in his important "triangular theory" of love.

In general, psychological topics within the intimate-relationship literature that are chosen for study tend to be within four general research areas. The first, *relationship processes*, deals with emotion, attraction, social cognition, communication, and interdependency. The second, *relationship challenges*, deals with stresses, power, conflict, and interventions. The third, *relationship development*, deals with attachment, friendship, love, commitment, maintenance, and changes over time. The fourth deals with *biological underpinnings* of intimate relationships. An additional, fifth, relatively small body of work focuses on sociocultural or context factors, including historical factors, that affect intimate relationships. These include cultural norms, gender effects, effects of sexual orientation, and cohort contextual issues. Finally, there are the clinical studies of cognitive-behavioral interventions and family systems approaches, both of which, as the names imply, focus on changing thinking to change behavior.

Although there are cognitive processes implied in these other four or five major intimate-relations research topic areas, the development or construction of relationship conceptual processes is seldom explicitly studied in relation to intimate relationships. In searching through the literature about intimate relationships, I noticed several areas where complex cognition (operationalized in my theory as complex postformal thought) is likely to be operating in some major way but is not likely to be addressed directly. Because relationships are complex self-constructing systems closely linking two individuals' cognition-related circles, complex cognitive problem-solving, reality-constructing, processes in relationships seemed important to understand.

Of course, every single one of the basic information-processing factors studied within cognitive psychology would be an important part of the cognitive system, whatever the specific focus of that cognition might be. Memory, perception, attention, learning, and all the others are involved in the epistemology of relationship existence and satisfaction. But the specific focus chosen in this book is closely tied to *complex problem-solving of ill-structured problems* and satisfaction in intimate relationships. Research presented in chapters to follow is from investigations specifically examining complex problem-solving cognitive operations and their role in intimate-relationship satisfaction.

Some categories of relationship processes, mentioned in the literature, that seem more closely related to cognitive factors include the following: construction of the self-concept; social cognition; beliefs about romance; communication; conflict; dialectical contradictions and turning points; and relationship maintenance. Some of these are being used in our studies.

The cognitive construction of the self-concept, with its intrapersonal, interpersonal, and transpersonal aspects, was discussed in Chapter 4 of this book and in Figure 1. The cognitive postformal construction of the self-concept can make sense of the models of attachment that individuals are said to use in intimate relationships. Individuals relate in ways that can be described to some degree as *securely attached* or *insecurely attached* with its subtypes of *anxious-ambivalent* or *avoidant.* The underlying roots of the attachment styles rest on how emotionally close individuals can allow themselves to feel toward others and how much they can trust significant others' availability and acceptance. Having boundaries, being able to attune with significant others without losing the self, and having low avoidance and anxiety lead to the best outcomes for relationships. The use of complex cognition, applied to the experiences of relationships an individual encounters, might allow for a balance between personal boundaries and attunement with emotionally close others that permits optimal attachment given any specific personal experiences. Individuals with complex postformal thought can construct a more inclusive view of the self-in-relationship, which in turn allows them to see that they have a larger number of possibilities for relationship while sustaining the self. Potentially, then, they can select the most useful way to experience close relationships.

Chapter 4 also relates to social cognition. Beliefs about romance are cognitive constructs in which construction of reality must be involved. Communication, of course, demands a cognitive bridging between two realities, realities that may differ, held by the two persons speaking with one another. If the cognitive realities are not congruent, conflict can be the result (see the application of chaos theory principles to cognition in "intractable" conflicts, discussed by Vallacher, Coleman, Nowak, and Bui-Wrzosinska in their 2010 article). Dialectical contradictions (demanding a cognitive "fix") during the course of long-term intimate relationships might occur when members of a dyad begin to "see things differently" from one another over time and begin to exist in two differing cognitive realities. Relationship maintenance is another, frequent, occasion when problem-solving judgments (and then behaviors) must be employed in a routine or strategic way to serve the purpose of letting a satisfactory close relationship continue.

In the research reported in Chapter 7 we will concentrate on the last context, examining complex problem-solving in the context of relationship maintenance. Our view was that individuals who were able to use postformal complex thought and who had satisfactory relationships would be more likely to use selected relationship maintenance strategies to keep their relationships strong than would individuals who did not have access to postformal complex thought. We also expected they would show better dyadic adjustment.

Postformal Complex Thought Operations as Applied to Intimate Relationships

In this section we explore just a few of the adult-life applications that make the ideas of postformal thought, with its association to felt connection, so useful for the study of adult development. It is worth re-emphasizing that cognitive development cannot be separated from its intersection with the complex web of felt connections that adults value. Postformal cognition and felt connection go hand in hand. A very early discussion of postformal understanding and the growth of empathy can be found as early as 1984, but further analyses of these ideas did not occur (Benack, 1984). For a reminder, look again at Figure 1 and at the earlier description of the development of this complex thought.

Let's look at the effects of developing complex thought on couple and family relations. The following are some complex postformal relational skills that will be discussed in this chapter.

A. The ability to recognize that another's point of view may be just as logically valid as one's own
B. The ability to choose a common definition of a conflict with another person holding a differing point of view or solution
C. The ability to understand that most relationship conflicts have multiple causes
D. The ability to realize there are always multiple possible solutions for resolving relationship conflicts
E. The ability to understand that more than one "reality" can be "true"
F. The ability to recognize in oneself, via feedback from one's partner, an emotional reality that is blocking relationship growth
G. The ability to jointly select one of many conflict solutions that reflect a larger reality that encompasses and respects the points of view of both persons
H. The ability to co-create a relationship environment that is favorable to ongoing growth because of learned skills that can

be applied to many relationship problems, rather than just one
solution for this particular conflict

I. The ability to understand the saving grace of joy and humor
and paradox

J. The ability to accept more than one method to reach a goal

K. The ability to make a pragmatic choice among several good
solutions

Just as individuals in the workplace must coordinate multiple
realities postformally, at least some of the time, if they are to succeed
in working together, individuals in intimate couples and in families
must do so too. We don't have as much success coordinating family
realities as we do coordinating work realities. We find it more difficult to bridge cognitive realities that are so emotionally important to
us. Intimate relationships are intense interactions, by definition, with
emotions weaving through each interaction and often contributing
heat to any light that cognition may shed. Framing actions of family
members in one cognitive context rather than another has implications for daily encounters and decisions, far more so than anything
that might happen on the job (unless work group is "family"). For a
couple or a family that remains such for a longer period of time, the
entire enterprise is colored by the history of past cognition, emotion,
and action.

Styles of dealing with this intensity are defined by the emotional
defense patterns, the shared cultural reality, the history, and the cognitive development of each person in the relationship. The presence
or absence of postformal thinking can skew not only defense styles
but also responses to shared cultural reality and the history of that
couple or family. Similarly, the emotionally based defense mechanisms, the shared culture, and the relationship history can distort
the development or use of postformal thought by individuals or intimate groups at later points in history. Further, these patterns are
taking shape within the psychodynamics of each individual, within
the individual's ongoing dialogue between the ideal and real self-in-
relationship, between members of the couple, in the couple as a
unique living system in its own right, between any of these "selves"
and society, and in the family as a living system. Note that even the
relationship itself begins to take on a life of its own, going on with
a history somewhat separate from the histories of the individuals

within it. It is as if additional layers of complexity were overlaid on "triangular" theories of intimate relations such as Sternberg's (1986) or Marks' (1986) theories, and on relational "stage" theories like Campbell's (1980), such that each triangle of relationship features or each stage becomes four-dimensional and transforms over time.

Researchers and therapists who discuss processes in couples and families usually tend to focus on only one or two of those several elements of the volatile intimacy mix, and then shape questions or therapeutic processes around that element. Sometimes the nature of the problem demands this reductionism; sometimes the therapist's skills are stronger in that area; sometimes there is simply not enough time. Ironically, when I focus on the element of postformal thought in this book, I employ a similar narrowing of vision, since I am looking most of all at a cognitive reasoning process rather than at some other sort of process. My plan, though, is to bring the discussion around full circle to show the interplay of *all* the forces as they are affected by and affect postformal thought.

We will start our discussion by examining the interplay and mutual causality of each of the main relational elements (which interact with postformal thought) just mentioned: defense patterns, cultural reality, and relationship history. How might postformal thinking help couples and families make it through life? How might their relational life stimulate the development of postformal thought? We will examine how these connections relate to marital and family harmony and distress. What kind of therapeutic strategies might become more common if we acknowledge the place of postformal thinking? Then we will summarize a sample of some path-breaking research on couple relations, a project initiated by Rogers (1989; Rogers, Sinnott, & van Dusen, 1991), in which postformal thought is taken into account as a factor.

Interplay of Postformal Thought and Other Elements in Intimate Behavior

The adaptive value of postformal thought is that it can help bridge logical realities so that partners in a relationship can reorder logically conflicting realities in more complex ways. This skill can let the knowers handle more information, live in a state of multiple realities that logically conflict, and become committed enough to a chosen reality to go forward and act, thereby reifying the chosen (potential) reality.

In an intimate relationship individuals attempt to join together to have one life, to some degree. As the Apache wedding blessing says, "Now there is one life before you . . . (so) . . . enter into the time of your togetherness." For a couple, three "individuals" begin to exist: Partner #1, Partner #2, and the relationship which begins to take on a life of its own. For a family, of course, there are even more "individuals" present, as family therapist Virginia Satir (1967) noted when she worked with not only the real humans present in her office but also with the remembered aspects of other absent relatives with whom the real humans psychologically interact. To have that one life together, to whatever extent they wish to have it together, the logics of the individuals must be bridged effectively. Those logics might be about any number of things, some of which do not sound especially "logical," including concepts, roles, perceptions, physical presence, emotions, and shared history.

Effects of the Individual's Cognitive Postformal Skills on Intimate Relationships

In some cases the individual has access to a cognitive bridge across realities, but not a postformal one. After all, realities *are* bridged, though poorly, if one person in a relationship dominates another and that one's reality becomes the other's, too. But this domination does not require a synthesis of logics, since one reasoning is simply discarded.

There is a variation, too, on this theme. Two members of an intimate union, because of religious beliefs or personal emotional needs, also may drop their own logics to give preference to that of the new "individual," the relationship, letting its role-related reality dominate both of their own individual ones. This, too, is not a postformal synthesis but a capitulation.

A converse scenario might find the reasoning of that third individual, the relationship, dominated and discarded by one or both partners' logics. In all of these cases that "individual" (the relationship) has been partly lost.

Members of the intimate partnership may find this winner/loser solution to conflicts large and small to be the best fit for them.

They may think the conflict too trivial, or may not be capable of any higher level solution, or may not be motivated to find it, or may not be emotionally ready for one. But *postformal* thought is not involved in this sort of resolution. As Maslow (1968) might suggest, this less skilled move simply might be the best move they can think of right now to deal with their situation, even if it raises new problems (in relationship terms) down the line. Perhaps this less skilled behavior is so incorporated into their shared history that it would be a challenge to their relational identity for them to have a relationship without it. But it is not postformal thinking, and it is less adaptive overall than postformal thinking would be.

Predictable Couple Problems When a Single Reasoning Dominates

When one reasoning system held by one of the two in a dyad domi-nates the other's reasoning, a chance for growth is lost. Emotional overtones also develop that begin to color the relationship processes and relationship history. The partner or family member whose rea-soning was dominated usually exacts a price, whether consciously or unconsciously, expecting a payback to allow the balance of power to return to the relationship. And less information can be taken in, inte-grated, and acted upon by an individual using one simpler reasoning as opposed to two different logics, or as opposed to a more complex single one such as postformal logic.

There are several predictable outcomes that are less than optimal when one reasoning dominates another. Lack of movement forward toward postformal thought slows the individual's growth. Having a single dominant reasoning begins or continues a story in the relation-ship history that is a story about winners and losers and simplistic cognitions about complex life events. It slows the individuals' move-ment toward understanding and learning how to work with the shared cultural reality (or the shared cultural trance, as Ferguson [1980] puts it). It does prevent any challenges to whatever emotional defenses the individuals may have used in the past, but keeps the peace at a cost.

A special case occurs if the intimate group is a family with chil-dren, none of whose members are using postformal thought. The predictable difficulties mentioned in the last section are multiplied in a situation with more individuals. It is harder for children to gradually learn a more skilled cognitive approach where there are no daily role models. It is harder for the children to grow up, create their own personal view of the world, and leave that family when power struggles centering on control of the family reality have been going on for so long in their own family history.

Benefits of Using a Complex Postformal Logic

Alternatively, the bridge across realities may be a postformal one. The incompatible several logical realities of the relationship then might be orchestrated more easily and orchestrated at a higher cognitive level to permit a more complex reasoning of the relationship to emerge. Postformal thinkers can adapt to the challenges of intimate relationships better than those without postformal thought because no one's reasoning needs to be discarded for the relationship to go on. For the postformal couple, power and control are not at the same level of threat looming on the relational horizon as they are for individuals without postformal thought who must worry about cognitive survival in their relationships. Shared history for the postformal intimates reflects the synthesis of cognitive lives rather than alternating dominance of one reality over another. Each reasoning difference or disagreement ends up being another piece of evidence that the relationship remains a win-win situation for individuals within it. This enhances the relationship's value and tends to stabilize it even further.

In the situation where one individual in the relationship is the *only* postformal one, we see a different opportunity and challenge. Several resolutions are possible each time an interpersonal reasoning conflict occurs. Perhaps the less cognitively skilled individual(s) will use this chance to grow cognitively, with predictable benefits. From my point of view this is the best outcome and one of the desirable features of having intense intimate relationships.

Alternatively, perhaps the increasingly aggravated postformal individual will let emotions overtake him or her and will temporarily resolve the situation by regressing cognitively and acting out against or withdrawing from others in the situation. This will lead to the previously mentioned predictable problems for couples using lower level logics.

Perhaps the more cognitively skilled individual will decide to wait and hope that the other(s) will come around to a more skilled view of the situation, in time. This tactic is easier for that postformal person to tolerate since the postformal individual sees the bigger picture and does not have to take the power struggle quite as seriously as other members of the intimate group. But predictable conflicts will still occur, and growth may be stalled.

A special situation occurs when this intimate group is a family with minor children. The postformal parent has reason to believe that the children will develop further and possibly become postformal thinkers themselves. The postformal parent might consciously try to encourage the cognitive development of those children in the direction that the postformal parent has mastered. After all, the postformal parent can "speak" both the language of the simpler reasoning and the language of the more advanced logic. The mismatch in cognitive levels will not be a cause for frustration, in this case, but rather for challenge and hope for the future development of the children.

The Other Side of the Coin: Effects of Intimate-Relationship Factors on Development and Use of Postformal Thought

The factors in ongoing intimate relationships which we have been discussing, mainly emotional defense mechanisms, shared relationship history, and shared cultural reality, potentially can influence the development and use of postformal thought, not just be influenced by it. For example, if an individual is emotionally damaged and is responding to all situations out of need (Maslow, 1968), that person is less likely to take a risk in a relational situation and let go of his or her own cognitive verities long enough to be willing to bridge to someone else's realities. Even the postformal thinker would not be likely to use that level of reasoning thought in such an interpersonal contest in which he or she is emotionally needy or "one down." Just as negative emotions often dampen the higher level creative spirit, emotional damage means the individual tries to regain safety before meeting the higher level needs of the relationship (other than those in which she or he is the nurtured one). Children in a relationship where the parents are damaged emotionally, or children who themselves are emotionally damaged, will find it harder to learn postformal responses to family dynamics. Such families function at the lower levels of unproductive patterns on the Beavers Scale, for example (Beavers & Hampson, 1990), described so well by Scarf (1987, 1995) in her classic books on the intimate worlds of families. The life-and-death emotional struggles that occupy such families prevent those children from having the emotional space or energy to bridge realities.

Shared relationship history also is a strong force influencing post-formal thinking. The habits of relating that individuals have developed in earlier years tend to perpetuate themselves over the lifetime. If those habits do not include postformal cognitive processes for relating at the time that a given relationship begins, and if many years are spent bridging the related individuals' realities in a non-postformal way, than it will be increasingly difficult for anyone (child or adult) in the relationship to move on to a postformal way of relating, potentially violating earlier habits.

An exception to this is the family situation in which parents may be postformal but young children are not. Postformal parents may find this cognitive discrepancy easier to bear than less cognitively skilled parents, but still will be influenced by living in relationships in which they are always using a reasoning level that is beneath their own. One's tendency to permanently distort perceptions about an intimate's reasoning skills, based on the cognitive skills they have shown during the history of the relationship with them, is very strong. We see just how strong when we see parents relating to their adult children as if those adults are still very young children. Parents must make significant efforts to overcome history, or at least reconsider whether historical patterns need to be revised, before using them to predict today's behavior. Intimates influenced by their history face an equally daunting task if they want to relate on a new (to them), more skilled, reasoning level.

Shared cultural reality (or social forces and roles) also influences the ways that postformal thinking can be used in intimate relationships. This is a domain where social roles often interfere with the choice of possible processes of relating. The shared reality of the social roles "appropriate" for various intimate relationships must be a "lowest common denominator" reality that the vast majority in a society can achieve, or pretend to achieve. The shared social-role reality for couples relations and family relations is often structured enough and at a low enough skill level that no bridging of conflicting reasoning realities is necessary at all. All that is necessary is to act out the appropriate roles in a convincing way and to make the socially appropriate comments about feelings connected to those roles. Tradition does save cognitive energy.

Notice that the first time in this discussion that we need to consider whether a couple or family is heterosexual or homosexual, legally married or not, childless or not, a May/December union, divorced or previously married, or with or without stepchildren or other relatives is in the context of this "shared social-cognition" element. Other than here in this context, the processes discussed in this book apply to *all* of these differing roles and family configurations. Only the shared social-cognition element discriminates among the various family configurations. Persons in all the various family configurations *can* use the same cognitive relational processes and can experience the same styles of relating.

A conflict may occur when the couple's views of the reality of a relationship come into conflict with the views of society about the same intimate relationship. This conflict might be the stimulus for the growth of a postformal way of seeing their relationship and seeing the world. For example, it has not been many years since the existence of a childless marriage was considered an ongoing tragedy, for everyone, and, if intentional, a sign of problems in one's personality and maturity level. Imagine a couple who feel very happy in their relationship, even secretly happy to have evaded the encumbrance of children, coming face to face with this tragic and stigmatizing view of their "selfish" childless life together and their part in the "problem." Knowing that such a view does not square with their personal knowledge may be the impetus for them to realize postformal elements of knowing, perhaps for the first time. The motivation in this case is social.

When the reality of one person in the relationship clashes with another's view, the intensity of the bond is what motivates them to seek a resolution. This is a push toward development of postformal thought, or perfection of it, since lower level logics will leave the conflict unresolved. Since framing such a situation postformally can help keep blame and anger at bay, postformal skills are often welcome conflict resolution devices.

The recent past has been a time of social change, especially in regard to the forms of intimate relations. While there are inherently limited possibilities for intimate-relation behavior in the human behavioral repertoire, certain ones of those possibilities are more fashionable than others at a given time. Living at a time of social change means that the individual and even the relationship is challenged to cross reasoning realities about itself without losing itself, all the while under shifting shared social-reality pressures. Access to postformal thought makes it easier for the social-change shift to occur while an identity is maintained by a person or a relationship.

Postformal Thought, Distress, and Healing in Intimate Relationships

You may have gathered from this discussion that acknowledging the role of postformal thought in intimate ongoing relationships might lead to some new ways of conceptualizing couple and family distress and some new approaches to healing distressed relationships. Postformal thought may be an additional tool for keeping relationships from running into serious trouble when the inevitable difficult times occur. But it may be the source of discord, too.

Looking at the bad news first, attaining this more complex cognitive level might lead to trouble and discord in a relationship. Imagine the case of a couple, neither of whom was postformal when they first became a couple. Time and the events of life passed, and one (but only one) member of the couple developed the ability to think postformally. This led to their each seeing the world and their life together from very different vantage points on many occasions, living different cognitive lives within the boundaries of their life together. For a couple that desires a deep level of closeness, this becomes a challenging situation; they no longer "speak the same language." Of course differences of opinion, differences in ways of seeing the reality of the world, happen for every couple, to some degree, at one time or another in their relationship, and their task as a couple is to grow through the difficulty and build a stronger union. However, in the case of a difference in the ability to understand at a postformal level, the couple has begun a time of profound and far-reaching differences in worldviews. The very nature of their usual realities is different much of the time; one sees it as concrete and existing "out there," while the other sees it as co-constructed and co-created through commitment to its reality. Even more challenging, one of the partners (the postformal one) can visit the reality of the other (the non-postformal one), but the other cannot yet visit back. So when one develops but the other does not, discord in worldviews may provide a temporary challenge (or a permanent one).

A second piece of potential bad news related to postformal thought and relationships is the type of pathology that may intrude when any unskilled behavior becomes unskilled in a much more complex, post-formal way. For example, if a couple is temporarily waging a power struggle with one another, they have access to a far broader range of strategies to do so if they are postformal, since weapons like sarcastic remarks can be used at several levels of the argument. In spite of these negative possibilities, it has been my impression that the positive features which postformal thought might bring to a relationship difficulty far outweigh the negative ones. In a time of conflict, members of a couple have to handle emotions and deal with their individual unskilled behaviors. If they can do so looking from an overarching reasoning vantage point that gives them "the big picture," it is easier for them to gain perspective on their individual problems and avoid blaming each other. They can weather the changes in the developing relationship better than the members of the non-postformal couple who see the world in polarized terms.

Application: Gender Roles

Let's look at one practical area of life in intimate relations where post-formal thought may make a difference: the roles related to gender (sex roles, sex role stereotypes) and behavior related to those mas-culine/feminine roles. I have written about this topic rather exten-sively in the past, and have included it in my research efforts because gender roles and the co-creation of social roles have been a central aspect of historically recent social changes in the United States (e.g., Cavanaugh, Kramer, Sinnott, Camp, & Markley, 1985; Sinnott, 1977, 1982, 1984a, b, 1986a, b, 1987, 1993a, b; Sinnott, Block, Grambs, Gaddy, & Davidson, 1980; Windle & Sinnott, 1985). "Gender role" is a different concept than sexual identity, sexuality, or masculine and feminine behavior. Gender roles may at various times be ambiguous, polarized into opposites, synthesized into an androgynous larger version, reversed, or transcended entirely. The general age-related progression of gender role development in recent history in Western cultures is from polarizing masculine and feminine roles to transcending roles entirely in favor of giving energy to other parts of identity. Gender-related roles enter discussions of intimate relations because couples tend to divide the work of living together, and gender has often been used by society to define roles. So couples enter relationships, even homosexual ones, with ideas of what proper socially dictated masculine and feminine behavior is. Sometimes identity is challenged when there is conflict over role-related behavior, making an apparently simple negotiation over something concrete like housework into a complex, full-blown struggle over identity and worth. If a couple is struggling about gender role–related behavior, postformal thought makes it easier to sort things out. A postformal partner can readily understand that, if he or she gets beyond emotional or habitual reactions, the roles can be validly co-constructed by both partners in any number of ways, as reasoning systems to which they commit themselves and weave into their lives. That partner can also understand that a gender role and its related behavior is only a minor part of his or her constantly transforming identity and is a poor index of personal worth. For the postformal partner(s) the negotiation then moves back to the domain of "what job do I want?" rather than remaining in the domain of identity and worth "I'm a terrible person if you make more money (less money) than I do, and my identity is in danger."

In terms of doing therapy with a postformal couple or with the members of a couple in which at least one partner is postformal, their level of cognition can be a real asset or a real drawback. The couple that understands that they are co-creators of the reality of their relationship, to some degree, finds it easier to open to possibilities and to change, in spite of history. They already feel that power and choice are partly in their hands, and that taking action is part of creating something new. They know that partners seldom have absolute characteristics that are not modifiable. Given the motivation to reduce pain and create a better shared relationship, and that motivation is the crucial part, progress is made with comparative ease. If the motivation is to obstruct change, though, the postformal thinker can create more ways to avoid real consideration of issues than other clients, all things being equal. Defenses can be more sophisticated.

Such defenses cut across several types of psychological problems (e.g., Sinnott, 2009a).

Postformal thought has appeared to be useful in connecting persons to others outside the self, useful for individual growth through relationships. The development of this ability might readily be facilitated within the approaches of therapies such as cognitive-behavioral therapy and family systems therapy.

7

Cognition and Fundamental Complex Relationship Skills

Some Preliminary Quantitative and Qualitative Research

L OOKING ESPECIALLY AT THOSE COMPLEX COGNITIVE FACTORS discussed in earlier chapters, why do some relationships last and others crumble? Why are some relationships satisfying while others are not? Does complex postformal problem-solving ability help create a strong relationship that can overcome daily pressures and "ordinary issues"? It seems reasonable that complex postformal thought gives individuals additional cognitive skills that help long-term relationships become satisfying. For example, if partners possess the ability to step back and view problematic situations as having many different dimensions that can be solved with several reasoning solutions, they are more likely to find satisfaction in interactions over time with another person who might see things differently on

Note: Undergraduate research team members contributing to this research and chapter include (in alphabetical order): Travis Geissler, Shelby Hilton, Jen Merson, Ana Nardini, Rachel Newman, Alyssa Probst, Ryan Schluter, Emily Spanos, and Corie Tippett.

some occasions. Humans have the incredible gift to communicate on a deeper level, and humans do crave these deeper and more complex relationships. Might this particular cognitive ability help facilitate individuals' positive experiences in these relationships?

Over the last several years we have been engaging in a series of studies examining these questions. This research program is ongoing and expanding. The details of the studies will appear in research reports in peer-reviewed psychology journals, but some basic preliminary empirical work is described in this chapter.

To test whether complex postformal problem-solving relates to style and satisfaction in sustained relationships, we used five types of measures in this first set of studies: postformal thought scales; routine and strategic maintenance scales; relationship style measures; the Dyadic Adjustment Inventory, and semi-structured interviews. In *Study 1* only the postformal and relationship style scales were administered and scale scores were compared with each other. In *Study 2* all the scales were administered and compared with each other. In *Study 3* in-depth interviews were conducted to see whether satisfied long-term intimates expressed behavior that indicated they were using the complex postformal cognitive operations.

Postformal Thought Construct as Operationalized in Studies 1, 2, and 3

Relationship satisfaction has been measured in relation to both cognition and behavior. Clearly the broad array of all component cognitive processes occurs within relationships, but what particular kinds of complex thought processes might especially *aid* in relationship satisfaction? Intelligence, as assessed by IQ tests, does not seem to be a cognitive factor positively related to complex postformal thinking ability (Hilton et al., 2013 and in press; Stanovich, West, & Toplak, 2013).

Formal thought processes are more geared toward scientific-reasoning ways of thinking. Just as a math problem of $2 + 2 = 4$ has only one correct outcome, logical (formal) thought implies that one "correct" outcome or answer always exists for relational "logical" problems as well. Formal thought is more specialized for solving well-structured problems in a scientific sort of logical way.

If a couple has a problem, a member of the pair who prefers a more formal thought process would take the problem at hand and seek the well-structured logically "correct" solution. However, a member of the pair utilizing more complex reasoning thought processes (post-formal thought) could have a more flexible way of perceiving "correctness" based on seeing the problem as an ill-structured or "fuzzy set" problem. For instance, a complex thinker would be more oriented toward finding the roots of the problem. This person would also see that there are often multiple causes for a problem, as well as multiple solutions for the problem. Complex thought takes the paradoxes of life into consideration in solutions.

For example, in the situation of infidelity within a couple, this difference between postformal and formal thought might be seen. Formal thinkers would be likely to either end the relationship or seek to work their way past the betrayal by denying that there really was one. The infidelity could be seen in one concrete way, perhaps as a betrayal (the problem), after which the solution would be concrete as well: either end the relationship or forgive and forget. Someone with more complex thinking could also see the unfaithfulness as a betrayal but could look past the cheating to see the possible causes. Why did the person cheat? Were they dissatisfied because the relationship lacked some key quality? Complex thinkers would look for the problem(s) that caused the betrayal, not just the betrayal as the main problem. The solutions would then be as numerous as the possible causes for the infidelity. Seeking the root of problems, emotions, or actions may indeed be a key to satisfaction of relationships since it honors the complexity of the dynamic system.

Such levels of awareness and consciousness of thoughts and feelings may allow access to realization of the "shades of gray" in life, as seen with complex thinking. Tuning into the dynamics of why things flow the way they do within a given relationship may be a means to achieving satisfaction. The ability to identify one's emotional states as non-absolute and effectively communicate them is an important part of managing the "truth" of the moment. Those who are able to first identify the emotions they are experiencing in a sensitive way, for example, discerning feelings of hurt or anger, can create a greater and more adaptive array of options for expressing their wishes to their partners.

The concept of mindfulness could be considered an aspect of complex thought. Mindfulness is the direction of attention toward one's ongoing present experience in a manner with curiosity, openness, and acceptance. Through repeated observation of thoughts coming and going through the mind, individuals may gain insight into their own conscious processes, particularly the transitory nature of thoughts and feelings with their non-absolute nature. Mindfulness has been found to be conducive to satisfaction in intimate relationships (Burpee & Langer, 2005).

There is little research that attempts to introduce a link between postformal thought (or cognition in general) and relationship satisfaction. Previous studies briefly touch on a possible relation but never explore it as the main focus. This current series of studies looks directly into the possible correlation between postformal thought and relationship satisfaction. Does the ability to take into account the knowledge that life consists of inconsistencies and multiple solutions to problems offer a tool for making a relationship more satisfactory? Dichotomous thinking could very well be holding couples back in relationship satisfaction. Commons and Ross (2008) feel that when postformal thought is utilized, blaming is reduced as relationships are conducted and viewed in more equitable terms. Commons and Ross (2008) go on to state that conflicts are addressed within larger, depersonalized frameworks of dialogues to construct workable solutions. Using complex cognitive processes may be the key to solving disputes between couples and may even lessen the number of arguments as well. Complex thinking could also be applied to alleviating boredom within a relationship; instead of breaking up, couples could rekindle excitement with more multidimensional thinking.

But, contrary to expectations, relationship satisfaction was not related to problem-solving ability in one study of older couples (Hoppmann & Blanchard-Fields, 2011). The key determinant in that study was the context of the problem. In the research reported here, we attempted to constrain the problem context variable to focus on problem-solving within the relationship itself.

The current overarching research question is whether complex thought relates to satisfaction in intimate relationships via use of intimate relationship problem-solving skills. Previous studies have touched briefly on possible links and have shown some promising theories. Reasoning and observation show that more complex ways of thinking assist in dealing with life's problems. Since complex thought can be applied to all aspects of life, it was hypothesized that relationship satisfaction and complex thought are positively related.

The ability to use postformal thought was tested using a 10-point scale used in earlier research and two new expanded scales. See Appendices 1 and 4, respectively, for the original and revised Postformal Thought Scales. This measure has been discussed throughout this book.

Overview of Additional Measures

Of the many additional measures we are examining in this extended program of research on postformal thought and relationship satisfaction, a few were selected for preliminary study. Those preliminary results are reported here.

Relationship Quality Construct and Measure Used in Studies 1 and 2

To examine this construct, we created a 25-item scale that posed questions about problem-solving within the relationship context. See Appendix 1 for this scale. The goal was to look at various applications of the operations of postformal thought in an intimate-couple context. This constrained the context of the discussion, which helped control the context issues found by Hoppmann and Blanchard-Fields (2011). The questions leaned on the operations defined within postformal thought, sometimes using the words reflecting the operation themselves. For example, one question gives a situation and then says, "When this happens to me, I define the problem and find several causes." The respondent answers in terms of a continuum ranging from "Completely disagree" on through "Completely agree." Other items do not use the words of the postformal operations—for example, "I see that, taken together, perhaps there is something in both sides of an argument." Another example would be, "I feel that my relationship has changed for the better." The relationship quality scale reflects overall complex problem-solving skills and satisfaction within the relationship and can be compared with respondents' answers about using complex problem-solving postformal operations in general.

These first two scales were administered in both Study 1 and Study 2 so that the characteristics of the relationship quality scale and the reliability of relationships between the scales could be estimated.

The relationship quality construct and measure were examined for reliability and validity.

Strategic Maintenance Questionnaire Used in Study 2

Previous research has dealt with some effects of maintenance on long-term relationships. We decided to explore strategic and routine maintenance as they relate to postformal complex thought and relational satisfaction. See Appendix 2 for this scale.

Relational maintenance refers to behaviors used to keep a relationship in a specified state or condition (Dindia & Canary, 1993). As Duck (1986) has noted, in most relationships the majority of time and effort is spent maintaining, rather than beginning or ending, the relationship. Aylor and Dainton (2004) also studied behaviors used to maintain relationships. Stafford and Canary (1991) created a popular qualitative assessment of maintenance behaviors that includes both strategic and routine maintenance behaviors. The scale used five relational maintenance strategies, or approaches, to keeping the relationship in a satisfactory condition. These five strategies are *positivity* (making interactions cheerful and pleasant), *openness* (direct discussions about one's own feelings and about the relationship), *assurances* (implicitly or explicitly reassuring the partner about the future of the relationship), *networks* (relying on the support and love of family and friends), and *sharing tasks* (performing tasks the partners jointly face). Stafford, Dainton, and Hass (2000) say that a mixture of both strategic and routine maintenance behaviors best achieves relational maintenance. They define "strategic maintenance behaviors as those which individuals enact with the conscious intent of preserving or improving the relationship" (Stafford et al., 2000, p. 307). "Routine behaviors, on the other hand, are those that people perform that foster relational maintenance more in the manner of a 'by-product'" (Stafford et al., 2000, p. 307). Duck (1986) also believes that a mixture of both routine and strategic maintenance play a role in successful long-term relationships. Although Stafford et al. (2000) developed this scale, the question of which type of maintenance strategy was most useful was left unanswered.

Using this concept, we created a Strategic Relationship Maintenance Scale to determine the degree to which strategic vs. routine maintenance was used by respondents. We hypothesized that the complex postformal problem-solver would be more likely to use strategic maintenance strategies to keep a relationship strong and satisfying. We hypothesized that a higher use of strategic maintenance strategies would be positively related to relationship satisfaction and to dyadic adjustment.

Dyadic Adjustment Scale Used in Study 2

The Dyadic Adjustment Scale (DAS) is a measure of the quality of adult close dyadic relationships (Spanier, 1998). Its purpose is to measure degrees of adjustment within the relationship. There are 32 items to which the respondent answers in a range from "Always Agree" to "Never Agree." The DAS includes four conceptual subscales: Consensus, Satisfaction, Cohesion, and Affectional Expression. The total dyadic score is calculated by summing the scores for the four subscales. The test takes 5 to 10 minutes to answer. It is not necessary to administer the test to both partners in a dyad; one member may be the respondent. The *DAS Users' Manual* (Spanier, 1989) contains case studies, psychometric information, normative data, and details about the development of the scale.

Interview Questions Used in Study 3

The interview questions were based on the Relationship Quality Measure used in Studies 1 and 2. The relationship quality scale reflects overall complex problem-solving skills and satisfaction within the relationship. See Appendix 3 for these questions. Interviewees were asked the questions that appear in Appendix 3, and their responses were followed up with additional questions as needed for maximum clarity. Responses were scored as to the extent to which they demonstrated complex postformal thought, using the coding system found in Appendix 3.

General Research Question and Hypothesis in Studies 1, 2, and 3

The general research question we sought to answer was as follows: To what degree and in what way does complex thought relate to satisfaction in intimate relationships? Previous studies have touched briefly on possible links and have shown some promising theories. Reasoning and observation show that more complex ways of thinking assist in solving problems and making relationships work in many aspects of life. Since complex thought can be useful in improving many aspects of daily interactions, it was hypothesized that intimate-relationship satisfaction and complex thought are positively related overall, across methods.

Overall Methods in Studies 1, 2, and 3

Design

Data were collected at two different intervals, 1 year apart, from different samples drawn from the same population to test this hypothesis. First, in Study 1,158 students were given the basic Post Formal Thought Questionnaire and the Relationship Quality Questionnaire. Second, in Study 2, 124 different students were given the Postformal Thought Questionnaire, the Relationship Questionnaire, the Dyadic Adjustment Scale, and the Routine and Strategic Maintenance Scale. Study 3 used an interview format and postformal thought scoring system to examine evidence for complex postformal thought in ongoing, real-life intimate relationships. Study 3 used hour-long interviews, and only a very few respondents were questioned in depth. These studies were approved by the Institutional Review Board at Towson University.

Study 1

Study 1 Method

PARTICIPANTS

The participants were 158 undergraduate students (38 men and 120 women) at Towson University. Participants were recruited through the Towson Psychology Department research pool and then linked to the website Survey Monkey to complete the study. Participants had to be 18 years of age or older and in an intimate relationship for at least 3 months. Participants were given extra credit in their courses for completing the study.

MATERIALS

Participants needed access to a computer with Internet service. They were tested with the basic Postformal Thought Questionnaire and the Relationship Quality Questionnaire.

PROCEDURE

When participants signed onto the research pool, they were given a consent form. Next, participants filled out a short demographic survey. Then participants were asked to fill out the basic Postformal Thought Questionnaire. Lastly, participants were asked to fill out the Relationship Quality Questionnaire.

Study 1 Results

The data were analyzed using a linear regression of each person's total scores on the two questionnaires. In the linear regression output, questionnaire total scores were correlated significantly and positively (r (156) = .200, p (one-tailed) = .006). Presentation of the item-by-item correlations, and a factor analysis of the scales, will be available in future, more detailed publications. A portion of these results was presented at the Association for Psychological Science Convention in 2013 (Sinnott et al., 2013).

Study 1 Discussion

The results from undergraduate Towson University students showed that the two questionnaires tested in this study are significantly positively correlated, as hypothesized. The total scores obtained on the basic Post Formal Thought Questionnaire significantly positively correlated with the total scores obtained on the Relationship Quality Questionnaire. Complex postformal problem-solving ability was found in those respondents experiencing and reporting positive intimate relationship quality.

The purpose of the first study was to find out if there was a positive correlation between postformal thought and relationship behaviors that work toward the satisfaction of the relationship. In the first study, we used the Relationship Quality Questionnaire and the basic

Postformal Thought Questionnaire. We found that our hypothesis was supported, showing a positive correlation between the two.

Some factors that could have negatively affected our results, preventing the correlations from being even higher, include the young age of participants, the inability to be certain that individuals were being truthful, and the limited number of participants. We also settled on an operational definition of 3 months' time for an ongoing intimate relationship in this undergraduate sample. In spite the possible extraneous variation caused by these factors, our hypothesis was supported.

However, we still wanted to determine whether the relationships found in Study 1 could be reliably found in a second sample. We also wanted to determine how the two Study 1 questionnaires would relate to a measure of strategic relationship maintenance, which seemed to be one of the few cognitively influenced variables suggested in the literature. Finally, we also wanted to relate all the scales mentioned here to dyadic adjustment as measured by the Dyadic Adjustment Scale. For these reasons, Study 2 was conducted.

Study 2

In Study 2 we hypothesized that once again the Postformal Thought Questionnaire total score would significantly positively relate to the total score of the Relationship Quality Questionnaire (Hypothesis #1). We expected to find a similar pattern to that found in Study 1. This would offer a second round of evidence that complex cognition was indeed reliably related to relationship quality and relationship satisfaction. We also hypothesized in Study 2 that complex cognition and relationship satisfaction would be positively related to use of strategic relationship maintenance strategies as measured by the Strategic Relationship Maintenance Questionnaire (Hypothesis #2). A final question was whether scores on the Dyadic Adjustment Scale would relate to scores on the Strategic Maintenance Questionnaire and the other scales. We hypothesized that they would be positively related (Hypothesis #3).

Study 2 Method

PARTICIPANTS

This study was approved by the Institutional Review Board at Towson University. The participants were 124 undergraduate students

(15 men, 109 women) at Towson University. Participants were recruited through the Towson Psychology Department research pool and then linked to the website Survey Monkey to complete the study. Participants had to be 18 years of age or older and in an intimate relationship for at least 3 months to qualify. Participants were given extra credit in their courses for completing the study.

MATERIALS

The materials consisted of a consent form, a demographic survey, the basic Postformal Thought Questionnaire, the Relationship Quality Questionnaire, the Strategic Relationship Maintenance Questionnaire, and the Dyadic Adjustment Scale (Spanier, 1989). The participants needed to have access to a computer with Internet service.

PROCEDURE

When participants signed onto the research pool, they were given the consent form. Next, the participants filled out the short demographic survey. Finally, the participants were asked to fill out the remaining questionnaires.

Study 2 Results

The data were analyzed using linear regression in an analysis involving the total scores of the scales. In Study 2, the Postformal Thought Questionnaire total scores and the Relationship Quality Questionnaire total scores correlated significantly (r (122) = .167, one-tailed p = .031). The hypothesized relationship between complex thought and relationship quality (Hypothesis #1) was supported again, as in Study 1.

A linear regression analysis was performed relating the Postformal Thought Questionnaire responses to responses on the Strategic Relationship Maintenance Questionnaire and the Dyadic Adjustment Scale, but there were no significant relationships. Therefore, the second hypothesis for Study 2 was not supported.

However, there was a significant positive correlation between the Dyadic Adjustment Scale and the Strategic Relationship Maintenance Questionnaire (r (118) = .518, p < .0001). Hypothesis #3 was supported.

Study 2 Discussion

The main purpose of the second study was to find out if there was a reliable positive correlation between the Postformal Thought Questionnaire total response and the Relationship Quality Questionnaire total response. Similar results were found in Study 1 and Study 2, suggesting reliable support for Hypothesis #1.

The difference between Studies 1 and 2 was the addition of the Dyadic Adjustment Scale and the Strategic Relationship Maintenance Questionnaire in Study 2. While these two additional scales were significantly positively related to each other, neither was significantly related to the Postformal Thought Scale. Apparently, they tap a different but consistent set of constructs, or at least operational definitions. We can speculate that the main concepts designed into the Strategic Maintenance Questionnaire (*positivity* [making interactions cheerful and pleasant], *openness* [direct discussions about one's own feelings and about the relationship], *assurances* [implicitly or explicitly reassuring the partner about the future of the relationship], *networks* (relying on the support and love of family and friends], and *sharing tasks*) reflect specific actions of partners that need not indicate a complex view of problem-solving within the relationship and might simply be habitually produced without thoughtful reflection. In the case of the Dyadic Adjustment Inventory, the main constructs designed into the instrument (Consensus, Satisfaction, Cohesion, and Affectional Expression) also reflect actions and feelings that do not demand complex cognitive problem-solving. Thus, the (potentially) habitual actions reflected in both the Dyadic Adjustment Scale and the Strategic Relationship Maintenance Questionnaire could correlate with each other without showing a strong relationship to complex postformal thought, a more clearly cognitive variable.

The results of one earlier study of couple relations and postformal thought may shed some light on our current results (Rogers, 1989; Rogers, Sinnott, & van Dusen, 1991). If the availability of postformal thought is related to the quality of intimate relations, we should be able to see an empirical connection between those two variables. Rogers set out to investigate the joint cognition of two persons trying to solve the postformal problems together. These two persons might be longer term married adults or strangers in a dyad, which might influence their cognition. Rogers also wanted to examine marital adjustment and social behaviors evident during problem-solving. She expected that well-adjusted married dyads would demonstrate more postformal problem-solving and more socially facilitative behaviors than the poorly adjusted married dyads.

Forty heterosexual couples between the ages of 35 and 50 were recruited for the study. They were mainly Caucasian, married for an average of 15 years, 75% for the first time, and 25% having had a long-term previous marriage also. Forty-one percent had bachelor's, master's, and/or Ph.D. degrees. After individuals were prescreened for intelligence they were tested for marital adjustment using Spanier's (1976) Dyadic Adjustment Scale. The individuals were randomly assigned to work in one of the following contexts: well-adjusted couple, working as a couple; poorly adjusted couple, working as a couple; well-adjusted couple individuals, working with someone not their spouse; and poorly adjusted couple individuals working with someone not their spouse. Then each "couple" (real or artificial) was videotaped solving postformal reasoning problems (not answering postformal questions on a questionnaire). Tapes were scored according to the coding schemes of Pruitt and Rubin (1986) and Sillars (1986) to obtain counts of the social behavior factors of avoidance, competition/contention, accommodation/yielding, and cooperation/collaboration.

While marital adjustment or dyadic context scores did not relate to using *formal* logical operations, these variables were related to using *postformal operations*. Eighty percent of the well-adjusted dyads (both real couples and well-adjusted members of couples paired with well-adjusted strangers) gave evidence of significantly more postformal thinking operations than the poorly adjusted did. This was especially true for responses to the problems with an interpersonal element. Analyzing facilitative social behaviors from the videotape, Rogers once again found that the ability to use formal operations did not relate to the social behaviors, whereas use of postformal operations did. For example, dyads without postformal thought demonstrated more contentious and competitive behaviors while problem-solving.

Rogers' results demonstrated that postformal thinking and adjustment in intimate relationships are positively related. Some generalized ability seemed to be present which operated, regardless of whether the spouses were working with each other or with strangers of equal cognitive developmental status. It may have operated by means of facilitating positive types of social behaviors and interactions, as evidenced by the fact that postformal thinkers produced more cooperative and fewer avoidant behaviors. Postformal thinkers seemed to explore and create to a greater degree, tolerate others' ways of seeing reality, and ultimately be able to commit to one solution. When working with strangers, they also took more pains to communicate "where they were coming from" in their views of a problem's many potential realities. Rogers' work suggests that postformal thinking (at least as expressed in actual problem-solving rather than as answers on a postformal questionnaire) is useful in intimate relationships.

This still leaves us with two questions. Do results differ if we test with a questionnaire (as in our current study) instead of with actual problem-solving (as in Rogers' study)? And does the ability to use complex postformal problem-solving develop much more slowly over time, concurrent with the development of dyadic adjustment skills?

The next step in our set of studies was to interview couples to find out how much individuals actually demonstrated specific behaviors tested in the paper-and-pencil Postformal Thought and Relationship Quality tests. Results of these explorations are presented in the section under Study 3.

General Conclusion for Studies 1 and 2

The purpose of these two preliminary studies as a whole was to demonstrate that there is a positive correlation between postformal thought and relationship quality and satisfaction. We found our hypotheses to be supported to some extent. But while it is very easy to hypothesize in the abstract, what can make a relationship withstand the test of time? Are these behaviors carried out just as easily as they are spoken about? Does behavior in real life demonstrate that individuals in relationships use complex thought in attaining satisfying relationships? This was explored in Study 3.

Study 3

The most important purpose of Study 3 was to see how individuals who were part of an intimate long-term relationship and who professed to be satisfied with that relationship would respond to interview questions about problem-solving behavior within that relationship. We expected that complex thought and problem-solving operations would be apparent in their responses and be positively related to relationship satisfaction.

Seven types of intimate pair relationships were considered for exploration in these interviews: heterosexual young adult married couples, heterosexual older adult married couples, young adult homosexual couples, older adult homosexual couples, adult sibling pairs, adult parent–child pairs, and adult friendship pairs. Of course, for all but the heterosexual couples, gender might also be a variable. While these interviews are ongoing, preliminary results are described below.

Study 3 Method

PARTICIPANTS

This study was approved by the Institutional Review Board at Towson University. Participants were recruited among friends, relatives, colleagues, and neighbors of the research team and formed a sample of convenience. Participants had to be 18 years of age or older and in the specific intimate relationship of interest for at least 3 years to qualify for this study. These preliminary results reported here are from only four individuals, ages 18–59: a member of an adult sibling pair, an adult child, a parent of an adult child, and a member of a heterosexual couple. They volunteered with the understanding that they would not be interviewed by anyone they knew and that their taped interview responses would be anonymous.

MATERIALS AND PROCEDURE

A structured interview was used. Responses to each question were followed by additional comments, probes, and questions by interviewers trained by the principal investigator with the cooperation of other research team members. The researchers created a list of 29 interview questions that were asked during each hour-long individual interview. The interview questions were directed at obtaining information about each specific relationship and the participant's thought processes regarding their intimate relationship. The questions were also directed to find out if each of the participants used postformal thought in their answers. During the interviews, the participants were also given three questionnaires created by the researchers. The questionnaires were designed to acquire further information on the way in which the participants viewed their relationships, and/or if they used postformal thought in their everyday life. The respondents were also given the scales used in Study 1, scored as outlined earlier.

CODING

The interview conducted was designed and coded to assess nine operations of postformal thought: problem definition, metatheory shift, parameter setting, multiple goals, multiple methods, process/product shift, multiple solutions, pragmatism, and paradox. The researchers used this postformal thought measure to look through the interview responses of each participant. If there was presence of one of these nine operations in any of the participant's responses, that participant would receive one point. This process continued with each of the nine operations of postformal thought. The maximum number of points for each participant was nine points, reflecting the presence of all nine operations in the participant's responses; the minimum number of points was zero, representing the absence of all nine operations.

Study 3 Results

The interview responses were coded and data were analyzed using descriptive statistics and linear regression of the survey scores with the interview analysis results. Although, with only four respondents, the correlation results were not significant, there was a trend in the data indicating that the interview results were positively related to the Postformal Thought Scale and the Relationship Quality Scale. This supported our hypothesis that interviews would demonstrate postformal thought in relationships that respondents consider satisfying. Results also provided additional evidence for the reliability and validity of the paper-and-pencil scales. More detailed exposition of the data will be provided in more extensive articles related to Study 3. The trends we found in our results indicate that it is likely we will obtain additional significant results when we are able to analyze data from a larger sample of participants.

General Conclusions for Preliminary Studies 1, 2, and 3

The purpose of our studies as a whole was to explore whether there is some degree of significant positive relationship between postformal thought and relationship quality and satisfaction. We found our hypothesis to be supported by paper-and-pencil test results. But while individuals might state on tests that they use complex thought in a relationship setting and have quality intimate relationships, how do they actually demonstrate these behaviors in a realistic life setting? Does behavior in real life demonstrate that individuals in relationships use complex thought in attaining satisfying relationships?

The three studies described here provide a first, preliminary, step in exploring these questions, and provide the first descriptive and empirical evidence for the positive relationship between the ability to use complex reasoning problem-solving skills and relationship satisfaction.

Of course, factors other than cognitive factors are important for satisfaction in ongoing intimate relationships. Cognitive complex problem-solving of a postformal sort is one part of the complex big picture of interactions that make intimate relationships thrive.

These results are only a preliminary first step in this area of study. Many additional investigations will need to be conducted before we can be confident in the support of our general hypotheses. In addition to continuing the studies summarized in this chapter, especially the interviews, other research is suggested in Chapter 9 of this book.

8

Cognitive Aspects of Close Relationships that Thrive

Practices for Dyads in Intimate Relationships

T HIS SECTION OUTLINES SOME BASIC ACTIVITIES THAT INDIVIDUALS in close, intimate relationships can use to create satisfying connection over time by using and growing complex postformal thought. Ongoing relationships provide challenges. What (on a cognitive level) might we learn to do to make things better? How can we practice these complex thinking skills?

The sexually intimate couple is often the only type of couple that comes to mind when we discuss skills and exercises for "intimate dyads." The exercises in this chapter are meant (unless otherwise indicated) for any of the types of intimate adult dyads considered in this book: close friends, siblings, parent–child pairs, and homosexual or heterosexual partners.

Note: I am indebted to Kate Price for her many suggestions for exercises and activities that would enhance complex thought in intimate dyads. Many of the activities presented in this chapter are adapted from her creative, astute suggestions that could form a book in their own right, and hopefully will do so in the future. Thank you, Kate.

This chapter offers an outline of activities that couples and intimate dyads can use, together in private or with a therapist, to improve their complex thinking skills and to learn to apply those skills to their relationships, with the goal of achieving more satisfying relationships. Some of the exercises are focused on the growth of operations of postformal complex thought in a relational context. Other exercises are applications of postformal complex thought concepts and thinking operations to make relationship events clearer to each participant. The postformal operations, described in earlier chapters, include metatheory shift, problem definition, process/product shift, parameter setting, multiple solutions, pragmatism, multiple causality, multiple methods, and paradox.

The activities described here are just a sample of activities that can be used to raise awareness of thinking operations that are useful for maintaining satisfying intimate relationships. In my experience, people are happy to practice the thinking operations, eventually adding them to their unconscious repertoire of relationship skills as it becomes clear that they enhance relationship satisfaction.

Sample Skill-Building Exercises for Dyads

Image Perception Exercise

This activity is designed to give participants experience with success in perceiving a concrete situation from two points of view. Participants can be shown a series of pictures that can be perceived in at least two different ways. Participants experience that only one perception can be entertained *at a time,* but that they can switch back and forth at will to differing versions of the "truth" of the picture.

An experience with the "paradoxical cube" may clarify the type of task that might be offered. Take a look at the illustration in Figure 3. When we examine this illustration, we may *first* see the upper-most square in front, as if looking up at the cube. But in looking at it a *second* time, we may suddenly be looking down at the cube, and the bottom-most square appears to be in front. The experience is only paradoxical when we, as observers, accept our conditioning and think that everything we see must be a three-dimensional object. Whether we choose the first or the second perspective, it will seem to us at that moment that there is no real choice, for when we are looking at it in

FIGURE 3 The Paradoxical Cube.

one way, it is impossible to see it otherwise. But there is yet a *third* way to view the illustration. It is possible to see an abstract pattern of lines with 8 points and 12 connecting lines. If the viewer is free from a predisposed assumption that the abstract form must be a solid object, and so is open to other possibilities, the absoluteness and the paradox disappear. Now the viewer can be aware that the abstract form has a *potential* of being a cube with both a front face and a rear face. The viewer is not locked in to either of the contradictory perspectives of the "truth" of the lines. Dyads can work with different types of these sorts of potentially paradoxical puzzles to experience the postformal reality of the co-constructed nature of "truth."

Pairs of Participants Play a Problem-Solving Game of Logic

There are multiple strategies of solving a problem experienced in games like chess or Master Mind or Strategy. Participants can see that the mental flexibility that they exercise in the playing of the game can be similar to the flexibility in thinking that they will need in resolving conflicts in relationships.

Case Study Analyses

Pairs of participants can be asked to read a case study involving a relationship conflict. Participants work together preparing a list of reasons why each person in the case study must feel and think the way they do, that is, "be right." Participants then can discuss possible options for conflict resolution, applying postformal thought.

"How Do I See You Seeing Me" Exercise

Participants can verbalize the (partially necessarily subjective, imagined) perception, of the *other* person's view of them.

Identifying Internal Conflicts

Defense mechanisms generally manifest themselves when an individual must confront a conflict within his or her own self, a conflict that has not yet been resolved. Working with a "danger zone" topic that evokes their efforts to avoid confrontation, partners can try to get in touch with the existing conflicts within themselves about that topic. Sometimes dyads are then able to see some version of these conflicts *in one another* more easily than they can see them in themselves. In an atmosphere of mutual support, partners may be able to help one another in making discoveries.

Understanding a Postformal Approach to Conflicts

With hidden conflicts brought to light, couples can be introduced to the postformal approach to reconciling differences. There can be a growing understanding that change can *only* take place through conflict, opposition, and bridging, all of which are unavoidable in human experience.

"Jumping out" of a Level of Seeing a Conflict

Einstein was reported to have said that a problem cannot be solved at the level at which it is first experienced. Dyads can practice looking at their relationship from a larger or higher level, getting more perspective on it. The "larger level" might be, for example, their shared philosophy that the relationship should last, or their spirituality. From that new vantage point the problem or conflict might be solvable.

Recognizing Postformal Contradictions

This activity is designed to help couples and dyads see that any identified "good" action or behavior is paradoxically a part of paired opposites, or contradictions. Interpretations and choices are made on a continuum and no single position can be held without consideration of the other pole of that continuum. Intimate dyads can be asked to discuss questions like the following:

(1) How much autonomy and how much connection does each of you prefer? No relationship can exist unless the parties forsake a certain amount of individual autonomy. However, too much

connection paradoxically destroys the relationship because the individual entities become lost. Too much autonomy paradoxically destroys the individual's identity, because connections with others are necessary to identity formation, differentiation, and maintenance.

(2) How much do you each prefer being *open* to other persons, to feelings, to experiences, to change? How much do you each prefer *limiting* the impact of other persons, of feelings, of experiences or of change? What are the ways this preference shows up in daily life?

(3) How much do you each want predictability or novelty? Examples?

Recognizing a Hierarchy of Problem-Solving Strategies

Using the following four basic problem-solving strategies as a guideline, dyads can discuss which strategy each uses most often to resolve problems. Does each person use the same or different approaches than those of their partner? The first three approaches do not make use of postformal thought operations and are limited. The fourth is postformal in nature and is more useful. Then the dyad members can try out other strategies to see how they feel and see how outcomes might change.

(1) One-pole dominance—Partners perceive the coexistence of both elements of a contradiction and seek to resolve the contradiction by making one condition or pole dominant to the exclusion of the other.

(2) Separation—Rather than legitimizing one pole and extinguishing the other, couples can separate the approaches over time or separate them topically. For example, they might alternate between contrasting poles from one point in time to another, or decide that one contrasting pole is appropriate for one domain or activity and another pole appropriate for another.

(3) Compromise—Like separation, compromise acknowledges both poles, but the poles are neutralized through compromise in which a portion of each contrasting condition is perceived to be sacrificed.

(4) Postformal—Partners might recognize the different dimensions, but no longer regard them as opposites. For example, the

party who ceases to regard autonomy as the opposite of connection and instead views it as an enhancement of connection has succeeded in reframing the contradiction in postformal terms.

Recognizing and Differentiating More Than One Point of View, Bridging

Recognizing more than one point of view using a specific situation, for example, "ways to spend time or money," can be an occasion for bridging from concrete or formal operational thought to postformal operations. Trying to recognize more than one point of view in an abstract situation (e.g., "what is 'loyalty'?) is sometimes a good opportunity to notice that there is no single "truth" about some relational concepts, beyond the one we mutually choose. Recognizing more than one point of view about the meaning of our relationship is another chance to note the relativity and the partly subjective creation of "truth."

Explorations of the antecedents of these different views may come from understanding our histories, including childhood loss. Discovering unarticulated differences and similarities can result in better understanding of the complexities of our connections with one another. Articulating those differences can lead to examining our current perceptions of one another and understanding what we want from each other.

Making a Commitment to Learn and Grow with Another Person with a Different Point of View

Making a conscious commitment like this is an application of the postformal complex-thinking skill of choosing the "logic" of our connection, what we wish to accept as "true" about our connection. Dyads can begin by identifying the points of conflict in the relationship, airing resentments and frustrations, and listening with intent to understand. More satisfying relations can then grow when the two individuals recognize that there is validity to both points of view, considering their varying histories. Satisfying resolution can be fostered by clarifying intent to understand and agreeing to commit to trusting one another's intentions.

Using Postformal Thinking to Resolve Emotional Conflicts within Ourselves

Sometimes learning to think postformally about our own inner conflicts can generalize to a more complex thought about our relationships, as discussed in Chapter 4. Members of a dyad can deeply question or become conscious of hidden perceptions that evoke emotional conflict within. The reality of those previously unexamined perceptions can be assessed. Then *choice* of the "truth" about individual identity can become more complex and be generalized to the relationship. The final step would be choosing more inclusive, realistic, complex perceptions about the self, more complete perceptions that can alter emotional responses within the dyad.

Using Postformal Thinking to Resolve Differing Points of View Encountered in the Other

The first step is recognizing the Postformal components within the conflict. When we begin to see this we can become aware that the resolution to our conflicts will encompass *both* of our points of view using Postformal operations.

One benefit of this understanding is the realization that building this combined new way of looking at our issues will provide opportunities for both of us to grow. The important "catch" is that we need to recognize that no solution will be "right" unless we are both committed to it and work to make it so.

Using Postformal Thinking to Bridge Commonly Held Attitudes that Might Obstruct Healthy Sexuality for Partners

In an intimate relationship that includes a sexual dimension, that dimension is subject to the same cognitive conflicts and potential growth toward complex cognition as any other aspect of a relationship is. Complex postformal thinking about sexuality can lead to a more satisfying relationship.

We often have surprising responses to discussions of sexuality. I've had clients occasionally who nervously worried that being a complex thinker about sex necessarily involved unusual positions, or acceptance of multiple partners, or Tantric spiritual practices. But complex *thinking* about sexuality is focused on beliefs, conflicts, and reasoning of who we are as sexual beings in relation with one another. For example, recognizing cultural barriers to finding a fulfilling egalitarian relationship *may* lead to our thinking in complex ways about the "truth" of our sexuality. Partners can examine polarizing stereotypes about sexual functioning, and then find their own "truth" about their sexual functioning. Partners can share their hopes and fears regarding the sexual relationship so that they might think in more complex ways—at a "higher" or more complex level—about who they are sexually and what they might enjoy. Together they can develop a postformal perspective in which meeting the mutual sexual needs of both partners is a greater good than, for example, following a rote script about sexual behavior.

These are just a very few of the exercises and explorations that intimate partners can use to explore, grow cognitively, and apply their complex postformal thought, with the goal of having more satisfying close relationships. I plan to develop a much more complete handbook of exercises for developing complex postformal thinking within intimate dyads of any sort. These exercises can be used by individuals with or without the facilitation of a therapist or a workshop.

In the next chapter I will suggest some potential future research. This research can involve the relationship explorations and exercises discussed here, as well as a few of the many unanswered questions suggested by earlier chapters.

9

Future Research that Includes Culture and History Effects

WE ARE JUST BEGINNING TO UNDERSTAND THE COMPLEXITIES AND possibilities for research in the cognitive factors that appear to be operating in the realm of ongoing adult intimate relationships, relationships that are evaluated as being "satisfying." In this book I have tried to stress the "big picture" of potential interactions in examining intimate relationships. The title of my most recent book is *Positive Psychology: Advances in Understanding Adult Development*, a fairly broad topic. Psychology's interest in studying these very complex relationships related to human behavior is comparatively new. There is nothing wrong with a reductionist approach to research, but it is time to balance that with a big-picture approach to answering complex questions.

Whether intimate relationships occur between spouses or partners, between adult siblings, between close friends, or between parents and grown children, they have a cognitive component. They must be conceptualized and integrated with the rest of our known reality, including the "reality" of the self. Individuals in all these types of intimate relationships share the necessary task of creating and re-creating an understanding of the "reality" of those close and ongoing bonds and life experiences that they share. They must, at some level, understand "necessary subjectivity," that is, that we, the participants, partly co-create the reality of those intimate relationships and of our relational selves. Yes, there are outside forces and factors that shape our experiences, and yes, emotions play a large part in shaping those relationships. But we always have a role to play in creating the "truth" of *our* lived intimate relationships. The sooner we understand that we have this role of co-creator, the better we can problem-solve in intimate ongoing relationships to help keep those relationships satisfying, by any definition we choose.

The way that relational understanding is structured, changed, shared, and influenced by culture and history (both personal history and global history) is important to the happiness and satisfaction of individuals in the relationship. The happiness and satisfaction of those individuals is important. But the larger purpose of creating stability in societies and maximizing the satisfaction, health, and growth of individuals *in a culture, at a period in history*, is also important. Satisfaction in intimate relationships impacts that larger societal good, just as that larger society impacts satisfaction in intimate relationships.

So far, what we do *not* know about cognitive factors in intimate relationships far outweighs what we *do* know. That is still a surprise to me. I began this theoretical and empirical exploration thinking that I would find a lot of theory and research related to some—any— aspect of cognition and intimate relationships. I kept searching one keyword or another, one lead after another, in cognitive, neuroscience, clinical, group dynamics, social-psychological, and developmental literature, thinking I somehow was missing some important scholarships and research about cognition and relationship satisfaction. Problem-solving? Constructing a self-concept? Meaning-making? The main thing I found was that I was being overly optimistic. My research assistants and I were not missing information; it just did not exist. I believe that we, as researchers and thinkers, serve our sciences best by addressing problems that are usually ignored, in addition to studying the details of phenomena about which we already have some information and theory. Exploring cognitive aspects of close relationships that thrive seemed like a wonderful, important, wide-open field of study, full of unanswered questions. This book is just the beginning of thinking about these questions and finding those answers.

When exploring a newer field of study, it is vital to create theories and to perform both qualitative and quantitative research.

As psychologists we pride ourselves in doing clean experimental empirical research, which is great. But that research must rest on enough of a theoretical and descriptive and correlational foundation to allow us to select variables that are logically causally related and most meaningful to our most salient questions. The research currently under way and the pioneering preliminary work described in Chapters 6 and 7 of this book honor this need to do all of theoretical, descriptive, *and* quantitative research in a new and evolving field such as this.

Individual Cognitive Development, Dyadic Intimate Relationships, and Complex Cognition: Many Circular Interactions?

Following are some general research questions to explore and test in the next phase of the study of cognitive aspects of intimate relationships that thrive. In the next few pages, I will suggest some targeted studies to address these research questions. The research questions in the subsequent paragraphs are organized along the lines of the following subtopics:

Extending earlier research presented in this book
Examining cognitive aspects of co-constructing relationship history
Examining subjective states related to relational cognition
Linking emotional and cognitive responses
Studying personality factors and their interplay with cognitive factors within relationships
Exploring self-construction within relationships
Learning about effective cognitive ways to enhance satisfaction in close relationships
Exploring dyad (and larger group) exercises with cognitive underpinnings that might enhance relationship satisfaction at multiple levels
Reexamining concepts within conflict resolution
Examining the cultural and historical factors intersecting with complex problem-solving to influence relationship satisfaction
Understanding the role of spirituality
Understanding the role of attachment style

Seeing relational dynamics from a self-constructing-systems/
chaos perspective

Integrating relationship satisfaction with basic cognitive
processes, such as memory and attention

Connecting relationship satisfaction to complex processes such as
consciousness, imagery, and intelligence

Finding the possible connection between cognitive neuroscience
and satisfying intimate relationships

Understanding the philosophical underpinnings of this approach
to epistemology

Examples of Possible Research Questions

Extending earlier research presented in this book

Interviews done with intimate partners could focus on what *they*
say brings them satisfaction, and how problem-solving does or
does not relate to that factor.

New, extended versions of the Postformal Thought Scales can be
given, relating responses to the other scales used previously.

Couples and dyads in relationships longer than the three years
(which was the criterion time we needed to use in our original
studies) might be tested.

Older couples and dyads, and those from non-Western cultures,
might be tested.

*Examining cognitive aspects of co-constructing relationship
history*

How do longer-term dyads describe and construct their "story"
or narrative?

Does satisfaction relate to the quality of their relationship history
"story"?

Over time, does the construction of the relationship narrative
relate to the individuals' descriptions of the "self"?

Does changing the way the relationship history is described
change the felt satisfaction with the relationship?

Examining subjective states related to relational cognition

Do self-attributions of dyad partners relate to their concepts of
the intimate relationship?

Do individuals' concepts of plans for the future relate to their concepts of the intimate relationship?

How do partners' constructions of their own integrative life stories relate to their concepts of the intimate relationship?

How does an individual's emphasis on the past vs. the present vs.
the future relate to that individual's conceptualization of intimate relationships?

Linking emotional and cognitive responses

What happens to complex cognitions about the intimate relationship when a member of the couple becomes emotionally
dysfunctional?

If an emotional state becomes more positive (or is interpreted by
a member of the dyad as being more positive), how does this
change the nature of that person's *process* of complex cognition about the relationship?

What is the usual range of *felt* cognition dyads experience in relation to parts of the personality, relationships with others, and
relationship with some Transcendent?

How does the concept of love (i.e., limerance or "romantic love")
interfere with or support complex cognition of and satisfaction
with an intimate relationship?

*Studying personality factors and their interplay with cognitive
factors within relationships*

What is the relationship between the Five Factor Model of personality and complex problem-solving in an intimate relationship?

Do individuals see themselves as having a consistent personal
"self" over the course of a longer-term intimate relationship?

Do individuals see their relational partner as having a consistent personal "self" over the course of a longer-term intimate
relationship?

How does personality shape the approach one takes to complex
relational problem-solving during the course of a longer-term
relationship?

Exploring self-construction within relationships

Do self-construction and construction of the concept of the relationship show similar complex cognitive processes?

How does the complexity of the self-concept change in the course of relational problem-solving?

How much and in what way does the particular concept of intimate relationships promoted by a culture influence the ongoing construction of the self-in-relationship?

In what ways does relational self-construction give feedback to influence the local culture in which the relationship resides?

Learning about effective cognitive ways to enhance satisfaction in close relationships

Can intimate dyads learn more useful relational problem-solving skills best from therapy or from practicing new approaches with couple coaches in a less formal setting?

What do members of dyads describing their relationships as "satisfying" *say* they do to understand each other?

What do members of dyads describing their relationships as "satisfying" *say* they do to promote satisfaction with the relationship?

Does learning about effective cognitive ways to enhance satisfaction in close relationships generalize to beliefs about effective cognitive processes in larger groups?

Exploring dyad (and larger group) exercises with cognitive underpinnings that might enhance relationship satisfaction at multiple levels

What types of these exercises are most useful to dyads vs. groups?

Historical shifts in expectations about dyad behavior and feelings often happen rapidly. How do individual dyads respond to that pressure?

Can certain relationship exercises such as those in Chapter 8, selectively chosen, be useful in resolving factional differences within a culture?

What degree of emotionality (emotionally labile responses) in a relationship defeats the utility of complex cognitive learning tools used to enhance satisfaction?

Reexamining concepts within conflict resolution

Can relationship learning tools be used to help resolve so-called intractable conflicts?

Which relational learning tools are most useful in conflict resolution during cultural conflicts?

How might conflict resolution practitioners reach conflicted parties in highly emotionally charged situations?

What are the characteristics of conflicts and embattled parties *not* helped by processes for building more complex views of a problem?

Examining the cultural and historical factors intersecting with complex problem-solving to influence relationship satisfaction

Have relationship scripts been the more simplistic model for intimate-relationship interactions during historical eras before our present era?

Will the current historical tendency to relate and communicate at a distance facilitate or discourage the kind of complex intimate-relational problem-solving that leads to satisfying relationships?

Will threats from overpopulation and the environment spur complex intimate-relational problem-solving or raise emotionality to the point where "cool cognition" becomes rare?

What sorts of religious beliefs support or short-circuit complex intimate-relational problem-solving?

Understanding the role of spirituality

Will the individual who creates a satisfying relationship with the Transcendent find it easier to use complex problem-solving strategies to promote relational satisfaction with intimates?

Does mindfulness training enhance intimate-relationship satisfaction?

Do individuals who *profess* a deep spirituality describe deeper and more satisfying intimate relationships?

How do individuals who characterize themselves as more spiritual cope with the ending phase of satisfying intimate relationships when those relationships must end?

Understanding the role of attachment style

Is it only the *securely attached* individual who can create relational satisfaction by complex cognitive means?

What is the best strategy for doing complex problem-solving relational exercises with *anxiously attached* dyad members?

What is the best strategy for doing complex problem-solving relational exercises with *avoidant attached* individuals?

If it is true that attachment style generalizes, can complex cognitive growth in an intimate relationship alter attachment style in other individual or group relationships too?

Seeing relational dynamics from a self-constructing-systems/ chaos perspective

Can cognitive style act as the hidden order underlying what appears to be random intimate-relational fluctuation?

What can be the "butterfly effect" in cognition leading to intimate-relational improvement?

Which perturbations of "settled" movements are best for promoting problem-solving complexity among intimates?

Do members of an intimate dyad see the "living system" of their dyadic relationship as able to change, or do they define change as the death of that living system?

Integrating relationship satisfaction with basic cognitive processes such as memory and attention

What is the role of working memory in an intimate dyad's construction of the nature of their relationship?

What degree of attentional focus helps intimate dyads understand and improve the quality of their relationship?

How does memory manifest in an intimate-relational setting?

Is incidental memory quality *negatively* related to intimate-relationship satisfaction?

Connecting relationship satisfaction to complex processes such as consciousness, imagery, and intelligence

How does intelligence (as traditionally defined) relate to intimate-relationship satisfaction?

How does intelligence (using new definitions such as "emotional intelligence") relate to intimate-relationship satisfaction?

Can *consciousness* of complex cognitive intimate-relational process be studied as a *trait* variable?

Might guided-imagery exercises centered on, for example, "meeting one's wiser relational self" be useful in improving the problem-solving approaches of intimate-dyad members?

Finding the possible connection between cognitive neuroscience and satisfying intimate relationships

Do functional magnetic resonance imaging (fMRI) brain scans distinguish postformal complex problem-solving from other cognitive activities?

Do electroencephalographic (EEG) brainwave analyses distinguish postformal complex problem-solving from other cognitive activities?

What are scan differences, if any, in the presence or absence of felt intimate-relationship satisfaction?

Do scans for postformal thought map onto scans of felt intimate-relationship satisfaction?

Understanding the philosophical underpinnings of this postformal approach to epistemology

Explore how the schools of philosophical thought deal with the idea of the co-constructed reality in the postformal approach to intimate-relationship satisfaction.

What philosophical beliefs about whether the nature of intimate relationships can be known might enhance or hurt intimate dyads' relational satisfaction?

Social, Cultural, Historical Factors, Cognition, and Intimate Relationships: Another Circular Interaction?

Theory building in future work also should include both consideration of cognitive aspects (e.g., understanding, problem-solving) and investigation of those larger social, cultural, and historical contexts in which intimate relationships are embedded.

Some cultures would not even give problem-solving a place of cultural importance in thinking about intimate relationships. Some would not consider "satisfaction" an important experience for intimates. While, historically, these cognitive and cultural areas of consideration of this behavior have been studied separately, actually, in real life, they are constantly interfacing with each other. A circular relationship such as the one seen in Figure 2 might describe this interaction. Research questions can be formulated on the basis of this more expansive theorizing.

For example:

How does the complex understanding of relationship satisfaction affect the creation and style of broader sociocultural, tribal, historic bonds, and visa-versa?

How do culture and the complex understanding of intimate relationships connect with or mutually influence each other?

How does the historical period in which we live relate to our own complex understanding of intimate relationships?

How does our own way of conceptualizing multi-person, or political, or societal relationships in the larger world relate to our way of conceptualizing our personal intimate relationships?

To Summarize the Overall Research Stance Taken Here

A larger circular interaction based on common cognitive and emotional interpretive processes about relationship is at work here.

I have *not* been trying to argue that understanding cognitive aspects of intimate relationships is "the secret" to understanding everything societal, personal developmental, cultural, or historical. Nor have I been arguing that understanding larger scale relational processes in society, personal development, and cultural and historical trends, filtered through cognition, explains everything going on for two people in an intimate relationship. What I *have* been trying to argue is that some complex cognitive processes may generalize in much broader ways than we typically consider. That common underlying complex cognitive process may describe an underlying order beneath the chaos of many types of relationships. Systems may work together and "feed" or amplify each other. So the processes seen in Figure 2 may operate in a circular way to amplify each other.

These are theoretical possibilities we can explore, by doing much more research and analyzing results using such tools as path analysis.

Appendix 1

Questionnaire Used in Study 1 and Study 2 with Demographic Questions, Postformal Thought Scale, and Relationship Scale

DEMOGRAPHIC QUESTIONS

1. Please indicate your gender.
   - ○ Male
   - ○ Female
   - ○ Prefer not to specify

2. What is your age?

   _____

3. Please indicate your enrollment status.
   - ○ Full-time student
   - ○ Part-time student

4. How long (in months) have you been in your current relationship?

_____

5. What is your sexual orientation?
   - ○ Heterosexual
   - ○ Homosexual
   - ○ Bisexual
   - ○ Prefer not to specify

6. Do you and your partner have shared spiritual beliefs?
   - ○ Yes
   - ○ No

7. How long (in months) were you involved in your previous relationship?

_____

POSTFORMAL THOUGHT SCALE

Please read each statement carefully and then select whether or not the statement holds true for you at all. Please select the corresponding number (1: strongly disagree—7: strongly agree) for how much the statement holds true for you.

1. I see the paradoxes in life.

○ 1	○ 2	○ 3	○ 4	○ 5	○ 6	○ 7
Strongly disagree						Strongly agree

2. I see more than one method that can be used to reach a goal.

○ 1	○ 2	○ 3	○ 4	○ 5	○ 6	○ 7
Strongly disagree						Strongly agree

3. I set limits to problems, but I really see those problems as more complicated.

○ 1   ○ 2   ○ 3   ○ 4   ○ 5   ○ 6   ○ 7
Strongly disagree   Strongly agree

4. There are many "right" ways to define a problem; I must make a final decision on how I see the problem.

○ 1   ○ 2   ○ 3   ○ 4   ○ 5   ○ 6   ○ 7
Strongly disagree   Strongly agree

5. Sometimes I solve a problem by finding a concrete answer; sometimes I solve it by finding a correct process to deal with problems "of this type."

○ 1   ○ 2   ○ 3   ○ 4   ○ 5   ○ 6   ○ 7
Strongly disagree   Strongly agree

6. I solve almost all problems using logic.

○ 1   ○ 2   ○ 3   ○ 4   ○ 5   ○ 6   ○ 7
Strongly disagree   Strongly agree

7. I tend to look for several causes behind any event.

○ 1   ○ 2   ○ 3   ○ 4   ○ 5   ○ 6   ○ 7
Strongly disagree   Strongly agree

8. I often see that a given problem has several good solutions.

○ 1   ○ 2   ○ 3   ○ 4   ○ 5   ○ 6   ○ 7
Strongly disagree   Strongly agree

9. I often have several goals in mind, and I try to reach more than one in solving a problem.

○ 1   ○ 2   ○ 3   ○ 4   ○ 5   ○ 6   ○ 7
Strongly disagree   Strongly agree

10. I can see the hidden logic in others' solutions to problems, even if I stick with my own choice of a solution.

○ 1   ○ 2   ○ 3   ○ 4   ○ 5   ○ 6   ○ 7
Strongly disagree   Strongly agree

RELATIONSHIP SCALE

1. Generally, I feel I respond to conflict when it arises in my relationship.

○ Completely disagree   ○ Somewhat disagree
○ Neutral   ○ Somewhat agree   ○ Completely agree

2. I believe my partner and I are equally equipped to solve the problems that arise in our relationship.

○ Completely disagree   ○ Somewhat disagree
○ Neutral   ○ Somewhat agree   ○ Completely agree

3. I believe there are some possible changes that might improve the problem-solving in my relationship.

○ Completely disagree   ○ Somewhat disagree
○ Neutral   ○ Somewhat agree   ○ Completely agree

4. My partner and I often discuss our frustrations and resentments.

○ Completely disagree   ○ Somewhat disagree
○ Neutral   ○ Somewhat agree   ○ Completely agree

5. Whenever my partner and I discuss our conflicts I find it most often affects the resolution process.

O Completely disagree   O Somewhat disagree
O Neutral   O Somewhat agree   O Completely agree

6. I believe my partner and I are equally committed to resolving the problems in our relationship.

O Completely disagree   O Somewhat disagree
O Neutral   O Somewhat agree   O Completely agree

7. I feel there are some issues in my relationship that are more difficult to discuss than others.

O Completely disagree   O Somewhat disagree
O Neutral   O Somewhat agree   O Completely agree

8. I feel my partner and I demonstrate some resistance when talking about things.

O Completely disagree   O Somewhat disagree
O Neutral   O Somewhat agree   O Completely agree

9. I believe there are some issues that are simply better not to talk about.

O Completely disagree   O Somewhat disagree
O Neutral   O Somewhat agree   O Completely agree

10. I feel that I often give up more than my partner in order to resolve conflict.

O Completely disagree   O Somewhat disagree
O Neutral   O Somewhat agree   O Completely agree

11. I feel that inadequacy exists within myself.

   O Completely disagree   O Somewhat disagree
   O Neutral   O Somewhat agree   O Completely agree

12. I see that taken together, perhaps there is something in both sides of conflict that are necessary for change and growth.

   O Completely disagree   O Somewhat disagree
   O Neutral   O Somewhat agree   O Completely agree

13. I can think of a time when talking about a problematic issue has helped me and my partner come to some agreement.

   O Completely disagree   O Somewhat disagree
   O Neutral   O Somewhat agree   O Completely agree

14. I have made a change in my relationship that has contributed to my own relationship growth.

   O Completely disagree   O Somewhat disagree
   O Neutral   O Somewhat agree   O Completely agree

15. Often partners disagree about how much they need togetherness versus individual time. When this happens to me, I define the problem, find several causes, and assess several solutions.

   O Completely disagree   O Somewhat disagree
   O Neutral   O Somewhat agree   O Completely agree

16. Partners sometimes are very open with one another and sometimes do not want to disclose secrets. When this happens to me, I define the problem, find several causes, and assess several solutions.

   O Completely disagree   O Somewhat disagree
   O Neutral   O Somewhat agree   O Completely agree

17. Partners sometimes disagree about the degree of novelty versus predictability they want in a relationship. When this happens to me, I define the problem, find several causes, and assess several solutions.

    ○ Completely disagree ○ Somewhat disagree
    ○ Neutral ○ Somewhat agree ○ Completely agree

18. When it comes to sexual compatibility I would say my partner and I are very compatible.

    ○ Completely disagree ○ Somewhat disagree
    ○ Neutral ○ Somewhat agree ○ Completely agree

19. I believe there is a lot of room for improvement in our sexual relationship.

    ○ Completely disagree ○ Somewhat disagree
    ○ Neutral ○ Somewhat agree ○ Completely agree

20. During sexual sharing with my partner I would say our sexual experiences are completely different.

    ○ Completely disagree ○ Somewhat disagree
    ○ Neutral ○ Somewhat agree ○ Completely agree

21. I have found that discussing ways to increase the pleasure in our sexual sharing most often is very helpful.

    ○ Completely disagree ○ Somewhat disagree
    ○ Neutral ○ Somewhat agree ○ Completely agree

22. I feel that my relationship has changed over the years.

    ○ Completely disagree ○ Somewhat disagree
    ○ Neutral ○ Somewhat agree ○ Completely agree

23. I feel that my relationship has changed for the better.

O Completely disagree   O Somewhat disagree
O Neutral   O Somewhat agree   O Completely agree

24. I feel very satisfied in my current relationship.

O Completely disagree   O Somewhat disagree
O Neutral   O Somewhat agree   O Completely agree

25. I would change certain aspects of my relationship.

O Completely disagree   O Somewhat disagree
O Neutral   O Somewhat agree   O Completely agree

Appendix 2

Relationship Maintenance Questionnaire Used in Study 2

RESPONDENTS WERE ASKED THE FOLLOWING:

Please select a choice that most resembles your feelings about each statement:

Completely disagree, Somewhat disagree, Neutral, Somewhat agree, Completely agree

ROUTINE MAINTENANCE ITEMS

I often ask my partner how their day was.

I routinely share household duties such as cooking, cleaning, budgeting, and repairs with my partner.

I prefer to show my feelings in small and subtle ways.

I hug, kiss, or tell my partner I love them in greeting, or in parting.

I find regularly sending cards, gifts, or flowers on birthdays and romantic holidays meaningless and shallow. (Negative)

I consistently participate in activities that my partner and I enjoy.

I repeatedly fulfill my duties as a partner in my relationship.

My partner and I regularly work as a team to care for and maintain the health of our pets.

I include my partner with daily decisions.

My partner and I make a habit of activities like praying, meditating, or attending spiritual events together.

We have favorite activities that we have a habit of doing every weekend.

I tend to have sex with my partner on the same day(s) of the week.

I don't like to help out if my partner asks me to do something repeatedly. (Negative)

I believe a good relationship can be taken for granted. (Negative)

Strategic Maintenance Items

I listen carefully to my partner's complaints and offer advice when asked.

I take time to plan outings and activities I know my partner will enjoy.

I find ways to let my partner know I appreciate them.

I strive to compliment my partner often.

I give up working on problems with my partner if they're being too difficult. (Negative)

I tend not to communicate with my partner because I feel uncomfortable verbally expressing my feelings. (Negative)

I would consider seeking advice to help maintain my relationship.

I take time out of my schedule to strengthen my relationship.

I go out of my way to surprise my partner from time to time.

I try to make my partner feel special.

I get satisfaction from trying to make things work out happily for my partner and me.

I don't think it's vital to understand my partner's feelings. (Negative)

Part of the pleasure of having a close relationship is understanding your partner's personality.

(For "Negative" items scoring is reversed.)

Appendix 3

Interview Questions and Coding and Scoring Guidelines for Interviews in Study 3

INTERVIEW QUESTIONS—PARENT/ADULT CHILD VERSION

(Note that slight differences in phrasing would occur in interviews targeted to spouse/partner vs. adult child/parent vs. adult siblings vs. adult friends.)

1. How satisfied are you with your current relationship with your child?

2. Are you quick to act on your emotions? If so, give an example.

3. When a conflict arises, what is the emotion you feel and does that influence the way you handle the situation? Do you have to work hard to remain calm and open-minded?

4. What types of different methods do you use to obtain a goal?

5. Besides logic, what are other ways you solve problems?

6. Have you noticed that your perspective can be different from others'? Do you feel that you are accepting of different perspectives?

7. How do you handle conflict? Do you feel good about how you handle conflict?

8. When you resolve an issue how important is it to you that everyone is satisfied with the outcome?

9. Where or how have you learned how to problem solve? Do you feel good about these skills?

10. Who would you say that you've acquired your values from, and how do your values differ from as well as stay the same as them?

11. Does the way you solve problems change when it comes to an issue you're passionate about? What methods do you use to keep your actions fair and in good perspective?

12. Do you use different tactics with conflict resolution within your family than those when the situation is with people outside of your family?

13. In your opinion, what is the best way to handle a conflict with your child?

14. Who handles problems better, you or your child? Does this have an effect on your relationship with them?

15. What types of conflicts have you and your child solved together and how were they solved? Did you feel happy with the outcome?

16. Is there an instance where you realized there was a different way you could have solved a previous situation?

17. Do you consider your child an important part of your life?

18. What qualities are important for your child to have in order to make you happy with your relationship with them?

19. Do you find it difficult to discuss issues with your child, especially if it is a topic you are not particularly comfortable discussing?

CODING AND SCORING GUIDELINES

Having access to any of these operations is evidence that the participant is shifting systems of logical reality to some degree. The degree of postformal thought shown by the participant is based on the nine different operations that follow. Each operation is one potential indicator of the use of postformal thought by the participant. In addition to defining how to code these nine operations, the scoring system is explained and examples are given, in order to clarify the coding and scoring system. The coding and scoring usually is recorded on a Postformal Reasoning Score Sheet.

Problem Definition

The coder should briefly indicate how the participant has defined the problem, listing the definitions. In defining the problem, the participant states or clearly implies that he or she is defining the problem in a given way, perhaps either as being a math problem and/or as a social relations problem. This is a labeling of problem type. It is possible for the participant to indicate zero, one, or more ways of defining the problem. Problem definition is one potential indicator that the participant can shift logics.

SCORING

Defining the problem in two or more ways gives the participant a total of one point toward "being postformal" on the tally for this problem and/or on the tally across all problems. Therefore, the coder counts the definitions and enters the total number. If the number is two or more, one point can be added to the total Postformal score, either for this problem or for the tally for all problems.

Metatheory Shift

Metatheory shift by the participant takes place when she or he clearly indicates that it is possible to define the approach to the problem in more than one *major* way, that is, in an "abstract" manner *and* in a "practical" manner. Both terms are defined in a standard dictionary sense. A response of two or more practical definitions of the problem (or more than one abstract definition), a situation that would have sufficed to get points for "problem definition," does not constitute a metatheory shift because metatheory shift demands a larger paradigm shift. The participant either voices that the problem might be solved in more than one way or actually solves the problem in more than one way, showing this major shift. The participant, therefore, is "labeling his or her *logic*" by stating that there is more than one way to look at the problem, either claiming it for abstract logic or for practical logic. The issue is whether or not the participant can shift between two different *logics* with different and contradictory implications for the solution of the problem.

SCORING

The coder simply decides "yes" or "no" in this portion, after listing the metatheory or metatheories used. If the score is "yes," the participant is given a point toward "being postformal" on the tally for this problem and/or on the tally across all problems.

Parameter Setting

Parameter setting involves the limiting aspects of the problem situation that are voiced by the participant or very clearly implied in the plan of attack used during problem-solving. These may be any limits or any variables that are set and/or used by a participant to describe the conceptual space in which the solution will be worked out. However, the larger dimensions of the logic and metatheory, or of the overall definition of the problem, may be taken for granted and left unstated during this (lower level) parameter setting. The participant is deciding the (lower level) rules of the problem-solving game. The parameters mentioned by the participant may be taken directly from the wording of the problem or may be added to the wording by the participant. Parameter setting must go beyond the mere reading of the problem, however. Parameter setting implies that the participant can increase and decrease the problem space in which the logic of the problem can then be worked out.

SCORING

The parameters that are expressed or clearly implied by the participant's attack on the problem are listed and counted. The listing of two or more parameters gives the participant one point toward "being postformal" either for the tally for this problem or for the tally across all problems.

Multiple Goals

The coder should briefly list the goal(s) that the participant has indicated. Goals may be stated verbally by the participant or may be implied by a clearly and narrowly defined approach to the solution. What is the point or goal the participant is trying to achieve? What is the participant's stopping point(s) after which he or she considers the problem "solved" (by any definition)? These are the goals. Stating multiple goals implies that the participant can make use of more than one logic about the problem.

SCORING

The goals are listed and totaled. The participant also is given a point for two or more goals. This point may be added to the Postformal tally for this problem, or to the tally across all problems.

Multiple Methods

The coder needs to list briefly the methods that the participant has used to solve the problem. The methods are the general processes and/or the heuristic that have been used to reach a solution. These methods are general in nature so they could be applied to any number of problems. For example, things such as formulae, multiplication, and addition are methods. General methods also include, for example, "seeking family counseling," "keeping the older person happy," and "putting foods together that taste good when eaten together." Sometimes "finding a method or a process that works in a lot of situations" is a *goal*, too, in the context of the operations called "process/product shift" (see next section) and "multiple goals" (discussed later), because the participant considers the problem "solved" when a good method has been found. As before, using several methods to get to the same end implies the ability to shift logics and commit to one.

SCORING

The methods are listed and the total number of them is noted. If two or more are listed, a score of one Postformal point is given for this operation. This point may be added to the tally of Postformal points for this problem, and/or to the tally across all problems.

Process/Product Shift

For process/product shift to be said to occur, there must be a shift in the type of solutions offered. With reference to those solutions provided, there must be at least one general process that is clearly seen as providing, in and of itself, a solution to the given problem. Therefore, in addition to a solution applicable to any of this sort of problem, similarly defined, there is at least one specific solution that would only apply to this particular given problem. So the participant with process/product shift (1) has clearly indicated the ability to define the solutions to a problem both in the sense of a generally applicable process and in the sense of providing a specific "product" solution, and (2) has shown the ability to shift between these two types of "solutions," one a process and one a specific contexted product. This ability implies the ability to select logics.

SCORING

The two different types of solution should be written down by the coder. The coder needs to decide either "yes" or "no" as to the presence of the operation. A "yes" gives one more Postformal point on the tally for this problem, and/or on the tally across all problems. Simply having a method and an answer is not sufficient (together or alone) for getting a process/product point.

Multiple Solutions

A solution is the answer that lets the participant reach her or his goal and stop solving the problem. If the participant acts as if he or she completed the process and reached a goal, but yet failed to voice the solution directly, it may be necessary for the coder to examine what the participant said or wrote. For example, the participant may have written down pairs of letters on the ABC pairs problem, yet failed to voice a specific number of pairs, after which it is clear that this array is viewed by the participant as "the solution." Yet if the number of pairs is on the scratch sheet, and the participant said he or she had reached a solution, this constitutes a solution. Creating *multiple* solutions implies that the participant can manipulate more than one logic.

SCORING

The coder lists all the solutions that are voiced and/or indicated, and totals their number. If the total is two or more, the participant receives a point toward the Postformal tally for this problem, and/or for the tally for all the problems in the aggregate.

Pragmatism

For pragmatism to be found, the participant must have indicated more than one solution and then have chosen a best solution or a "clear winner" from the solutions given, thus permitting him or her to move on to the next problem. There must be evidence that the participant was able to make a choice between these competing solutions or realities and, having made a choice, was then able to move forward. This implies access to postformal logic. Pragmatism in this application differs slightly from the usual definition of pragmatism found in the dictionary.

SCORING

The coder indicates "yes" or "no." A "yes" code gives the participant one point toward "being postformal" on the tally for a single problem or on the tally across all problems.

Paradox

Paradox, as an operation of postformal thought, is defined as a seemingly contradictory statement that may nonetheless be true. In this operation, the participant has noted that there is a contradiction present in the apparently simultaneous demands of the problem for (for example) simply looking for a mathematical solution and simultaneously creating a solution applicable to the real world. The participant appears to understand that there is a "double bind" quality to the demands of the problem. Often this brings out the participant's sense of humor. Awareness of paradox implies awareness of multiple logical contradictory realities.

SCORING

The coder scores a "yes" or a "no" for paradox on this problem. The participant is given a point for "being postformal" if he or she obtains a "yes." The point may then be included in the tally for this problem or the tally across all problems.

Appendix 4

Revised Postformal Thought
Questionnaire #1

QUESTIONNAIRE

Please read each statement carefully and then select whether or not the statement holds true for you at all. Please circle the corresponding number (1: Strongly Disagree; 7: Strongly Agree) for how much the statement holds true for you. After each question on which you answered something higher than 1, please describe briefly an occasion on which it was evident.

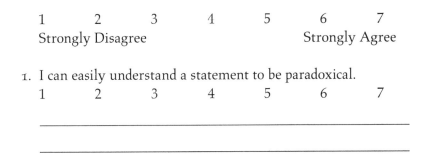

    1   2   3   4   5   6   7

Strongly Disagree   Strongly Agree

1. I can easily understand a statement to be paradoxical.

    1   2   3   4   5   6   7

_____

_____

2. I see more than one method that can be used to reach a goal.

   1   2   3   4   5   6   7

   _____

   _____

3. I set limits to problems, but I really see those problems as more complex.

   1   2   3   4   5   6   7

   _____

   _____

4. There are many "right" ways to define a problem; I must make a final decision on how I see the problem.

   1   2   3   4   5   6   7

   _____

   _____

5. Sometimes I solved a problem by finding a concrete <u>answer</u>; sometimes I solve it by finding a correct <u>process</u> to deal with problems "of this type."

   1   2   3   4   5   6   7

   _____

   _____

6. I solve almost all problems using logic.

   1   2   3   4   5   6   7

   _____

   _____

7. I tend to look for several causes behind any event.

   1   2   3   4   5   6   7

   _____

   _____

8. I often see that a given problem has several good solutions.

    1   2   3   4   5   6   7

_____

_____

9. I often have several goals in mind, and I try to reach more than one in solving a problem.

    1   2   3   4   5   6   7

_____

_____

10. I can see the hidden logic in others' solutions to problems, even if I stick with my own choice of a solution.

    1   2   3   4   5   6   7

_____

_____

11. I usually see only one way to reach a particular goal.

    1   2   3   4   5   6   7

_____

_____

12. I cannot recognize a statement to be contradictory and also be true.

    1   2   3   4   5   6   7

_____

_____

13. I allow problems to progress naturally, and I find the problems very simple to understand.

    1   2   3   4   5   6   7

_____

_____

14. No matter how I see the problem, there is only one "right" was it can be defined.

    1   2   3   4   5   6   7

    _____

    _____

15. I solve problems <u>abstractly</u>; I find that there is not one correct way to solve a problem "of this type."

    1   2   3   4   5   6   7

    _____

    _____

16. I solve almost all problems using my own ideas and theories.

    1   2   3   4   5   6   7

    _____

    _____

17. I typically can see one particular cause behind an event.

    1   2   3   4   5   6   7

    _____

    _____

18. I normally solve problems using one solution.

    1   2   3   4   5   6   7

    _____

    _____

19. I believe it is important to have one goal in mind, and try to reach that goal when solving a problem.

    1   2   3   4   5   6   7

    _____

    _____

20. I recognize the logic behind others' solutions to problems, even though I take the solutions of others into consideration.

1   2   3   4   5   6   7

_____

_____

Short Form Postformal Thought Scale

Each question is followed by the 7-point scale.

How true is this for you? (Circle one)

Very true			Somewhat true			Not true	
7	6	5	4	3	2	1

1. I see the paradoxes in life.

2. I see more than one method that can be used to reach a goal.

3. I set limits to problems, but I really see those problems as more complicated.

4. There are many "right" ways to define a problem; I must make a final decision on how I see the problem.

5. Sometimes I solve a problem by finding a concrete <u>answer</u>; sometimes I solve it by finding a correct <u>process</u> to deal with problems "of this type."

6. I solve almost all problems using logic.

7. I tend to look for several causes behind any event.

8. I often see that a given problem has several good solutions.

9. I often have several goals in mind, and I try to reach more than one in solving a problem.

10. I can see the hidden logic in others' solutions to problems, even if I stick with my own choice of a solution.

References

Abraham, R. (1985). Is there chaos without noise? In P. Fisher & W. Smith (Eds.), *Chaos, fractals, and dynamics* (pp. 117–121). New York: Marcel Dekker.

Acemoglu, D., & Robinson, J. A. (2012). *Why nations fail: The origins of power, prosperity and poverty.* New York: Crown.

Alper, J. (1989). The chaotic brain: New models of behavior. *Psychology Today, 23,* 21.

Aylor, B., & Dainton, M. (2004). Biological sex and psychological fenderas predictors of routine and strategic relational maintenance. *Sex Roles, 50,* 689–697.

Barton, S. (1994). Chaos, self- organization, and psychology. *American Psychologist, 49,* 5–14.

Beavers, W., & Hampson, R. (1990). *Successful families: Assessment and intervention.* New York: W.W. Norton.

Benovenli, L., Fuller, E., Sinnott, J., & Waterman, S. (2011). Three applications of the theory of postformal thought: Wisdom, concepts of God, and success in college. *Research in the Social Scientific Study of Religion, 22,* 141–154.

Benack, S. (1984). Postformal epistemologies and the growth of empathy. In M. Commons, F. Richards, & C. Armon (Eds.), *Beyond formal operations* (pp. 340–356). New York: Praeger.

Blauberg, I., Sadovsky, V., & Yudin, E. (1977). *Systems theory.* Moscow: Progress Publishers.

Bohm, D. (1980). *Wholeness and the implicate order.* London: Routledge and Kegan Paul.

Born, M. (1962). *Einstein's theory of relativity.* New York: Dover.

Born, M. (1964). *Natural philosophy of cause and chance.* New York: Dover.

Brillouin, L. (1970). *Relativity reexamined.* New York: Academic Press.

Brown, N. M., & Amatea, E. S. (2000). *Love and intimate relationships: Journeys of the heart.* Philadelphia: Taylor and Francis.

Burpee, L. C., & Langer, E. J. (2005). Mindfulness and marital satisfaction. *Journal of Adult Development, 12,* 43–51.

Campbell, S. (1980). *The couple's journey: Intimacy as a path to wholeness.* San Luis Obispo, CA: Impact.

Capra, F. (1975). *The tao of physics.* New York: Bantam.

Carter, B., & McGoldrick, M. (2005). *The expanded family life cycle.* Boston: Allyn and Bacon.

Cartwright, K. B., Galupo, M. P., Tyree, S. D., & Jennings, J. (2009). Reliability and validity of the Complex Postformal Thought Questionnaire. *Journal of Adult Development, 16,* 183–189.

Cassirer, E. (1923). *Substance and function, and Einstein's theory of relativity.* New York: Dover.

Cassirer, E. (1950). *The problem of knowledge.* New Haven, CT: Yale University Press.

Cassirer, E. (1956). *Determinism and indeterminism in modern physics.* New Haven, CT: Yale University Press.

Cavanaugh, J. C. (1989*). The utility of concepts in chaos theory for psychological theory and research.* Paper presented at the Fourth Adult Development Conference at Harvard University, Cambridge, MA.

Cavanaugh, J., Kramer, D., Sinnott, J. D., Camp, C., & Markley, R. P. (1985). On missing links and such: Interfaces between cognitive research and everyday problem-solving. *Human Development, 28,* 146–168.

Cavanaugh, J. C., & McGuire, L. (1994). The chaos of lifespan learning. In J. Sinnott (Ed.). *Interdisciplinary handbook of adult lifespan learning* (pp. 3–21). Westport, CT: Greenwood.

Chap, J. B., & Sinnott, J. D. (1977-78). Performance on institutionalized and community active old persons on concrete and formal Piagetian tasks. *International Journal of Aging and Human Development, 8,* 269–278.

Commons, M., Armon, C., Kohlberg, L., Richards, F., Grotzer, T., & Sinnott, J. D. (Eds.) (1989). *Beyond formal operations III: Models and methods in the study of adult and adolescent thought.* New York: Praeger.

Commons, M., Richards, F., & Armon, C. (Eds.) (1984). *Beyond formal operations.* New York: Praeger.

Commons, M., & Ross, S. N. (2008). What postformal thought is and why it matters. *World Futures, 64,* 321–329.

Commons, M., Sinnott, J. D., Richards, F., & Armon, C. (Eds.) (1989). *Adult development II: Comparisons and applications of adolescent and adult developmental models.* New York: Praeger.

Coontz, S. (2005). *Marriage, a history: From obedience to intimacy, or how love conquered marriage.* New York: Viking.

Crutchfield, J. P., Farmer, J. D., Packard, N. H., & Shaw, R. S. (1986). Chaos. *Scientific American, 255,* 46–57.

Devaney, R. (1989). *An introduction to chaotic dynamical systems.* Redwood City, CA: Addison-Wesley.

Diamond, J. (1999). *Guns, germs and steel: The fates of human societies.* New York: W.W. Norton.

Diamond, J. (2007). *Collapse: How societies choose to fail of succeed.* New York: Viking.

Dindia, K., & Canary, D. J. (1993). Definitions and theoretical perspectives on maintaining relationships. *Journal of Social and Personal Relationships, 10,* 163–173.

Duck, S. W. (1986). *Human relationships.* Newbury Park, CA: SAGE Press.

Einstein, A. (1961). *Relativity: The special and general theory.* New York: Crown.

Erikson, E. (1982). *The life cycle completed.* New York: W.W. Norton.

Ferguson, M. (1980). *The Aquarian conspiracy: Personal and social transformation in the 1980s.* Los Angeles: Tarcher.

Freedle, R. (1977). Psychology, Thomian topologies, deviant logics, and human development. In N. Datan & H. Reese (Eds.), *Lifespan developmental psychology: Postformal perspectives on experimental research* (pp. 317–342). New York: Academic Press.

Galupo, M. P., Cartwright, K. B., & Savage, L. S. (2010). Cross-social category friendships as a context for postformal cognitive development. *Journal of Adult Development, 17*, 208–214.

Gleick, J. (1987). *Chaos: Making a new science.* New York: Penguin Books.

Goerner, S. (1994). *Chaos and the evolving psychological universe.* Langhorne, PA: Gordon & Breach Scientific Publishers.

Goldberg, A. (2010). *Lesbian and gay parents and their children.* Washington, DC: American Psychiatric Association.

Goldstein, (1994). *The unshackled organization.* Portland, OR: Productivity Press.

Gottman, J. (1991). Chaos and regulated change in families: A metaphor for the study of transitions. In P. A. Cohen & M. Hetherington (Eds.), *Family transitions* (pp. 247–272). Hillsdale, NJ: Lawrence Erlbaum.

Griffin, J., Gooding, S., Semesky, M., Brittany Farmer, B., Mannchen, G., & Sinnott, J. D. (2009). Four brief studies of relations between postformal thought and non-cognitive factors: Personality, concepts of God, political opinions and social attitudes. *Journal of Adult Development, 16*(3), 173–182.

Haidt, J. (2012). *Righteous mind: Why good people are divided by politics and religion.* New York: Pantheon Books.

Heisenberg, W. (1958). *Physics and philosophy.* New York: Harper and Row.

Hilton, S., Spanos, E., Spearman, Z., Topel, R., Welsh, K., Wood, M., & Sinnott, J. D. (2013 and in press). *The relationship between intelligence and postformal thought when motivation is controlled.* Paper presented at the Research Expo, Towson University, Towson, MD.

Hofstadter, D. R. (1979). *Godel, Escher and Bach: An eternal golden braid.* New York: Basic Books.

Hoppmann, C. A., & Blanchard-Fields, F. (2011). Problem-solving variability in older spouses: How is it linked to problem-, person-, and couple-characteristics? *Psychology and Aging, 26*, 525–531.

Inhelder, B., & Piaget, J. (1958). *The growth of logical thinking from childhood to adolescence.* New York: Basic Books.

Jennings, J., Galupo, M., & Cartwright, K. (2009). The role of postformal cognitive development in death acceptance. *Journal of Adult Development, 16*, 166–172.

Johnson, L. (1991). Bridging paradigms: The role of a change agent in an international technical transfer project. In J. Sinnott & J. Cavanaugh (Eds.), *Bridging paradigms: Positive development in adulthood and cognitive aging* (pp. 59–72). New York: Praeger.

Johnson, L. (1994). Nonformal adult learning in international development projects. In J. D. Sinnott (Ed.), *Interdisciplinary handbook of adult lifespan learning* (pp. 203–217). Westport, CT: Greenwood.

Johnson, L. (2004). *Postformal thinking in the workplace.* Stockholm: University of Stockholm Press.

Johnson, L., & Sinnott, J. D. (1996). *Complex reasoning styles in expert research administrators.* Paper presented at the Society for Research Administrators National Conference, Toronto.

Jones, R. S. (1992). *Physics for the rest of us: Ten basic ideas of 20th century physics.* New York: Fall River Press.

Jung, C. (1930/1971). The stages of life. In J. Campbell (Ed.), *The portable Jung.* New York: Viking Library.

Kauffman, S. (1993). *The origins of order.* New York: Oxford University Press.

Kaufman, W. (1973). *Relativity and cosmology.* New York: Harper & Row.

Kelley, H. H., Berscheid, E., Christensen, A., Harvey, J. H., Huston, T. L., Levinger, G., McClintock, E., Peplau, L. A., & Peterson, D. R. (1983). *Close relationships.* New York: W.H. Freeman.

Kelly, K. (1994). *Out of control: The new biology of machines, social systems and the economic world.* Reading, MA: Addison-Wesley.

Kuhn, D. (1978). Mechanisms of cognitive and social development: One psychology or two? *Human Development, 21*, 92–118.

Kuhn, T. (1962). *The structure of scientific revolutions.* Chicago: University of Chicago Press.

Lee, D. M. (1987). *Relativistic operations: A framework for conceptualizing teachers' everyday problem-solving.* Paper presented at the Third Beyond Formal Operations Conference at Harvard University, Cambridge, MA.

Lee, D. M. (1991). Relativistic operations: A framework for conceptualizing teachers' everyday problem-solving. In J. Sinnott &

J. Cavanaugh (Eds.), *Bridging paradigms: Positive development in adulthood and cognitive aging* (pp. 73–68). New York: Praeger.

Lee, D. M. (1994a). Becoming an expert: Reconsidering the place of wisdom in teaching adults. In J. D. Sinnott (Ed.), *Interdisciplinary handbook of adult lifespan learning* (pp. 234–248). Westport, CT: Greenwood.

Lee, D. M. (1994b). Models of collaboration in adult reasoning. In J. D. Sinnott (Ed.), *Interdisciplinary handbook of adult lifespan learning* (pp. 51–60). Westport, CT: Greenwood.

Levine, R. L., & Fitzgerald, H. E. (Eds.) (1992). *Analysis of dynamic psychological systems, Vols. 1 & 2*. New York: Plenum.

Lockland, G. T. (1973). *Grow or die*. New York: Random House.

Lorenz, E. (1963). Deterministic non-periodic flow. *Journal of Atmospheric Sciences, 20*, 130–141.

Lorenz, E. (1979). *Predictability: Does the flap of a butterfly's wings in Brazil set off a tornado in Texas?* Paper presented at the annual meeting of the American Association for the Advancement of Science, Washington, DC.

Mahoney, M. J. (1991). *Human change processes*. New York: Basic Books.

Marks, S. (1986). *Three corners: Exploring marriage and the self*. Lexington, MA: D.C. Heath & Company.

Maslow, A. H. (1968). *Toward a psychology of being*. New York: Van Nostrand Reinhold.

Maturana, H., & Varela, F. (1980). *Autopoiesis and cognition: The realization of the living*. Boston: D. Reidel.

McAdams, D. P. (2013). The psychological self as actor, agent, and author. *Psychological Science, 8*, 272–295.

Merchant, L. (2012). *Adult cognition, creativity, and political ideology*. Manuscript submitted for review. Master's thesis, Towson University, Towson, MD.

Miller, J. (1978). *Living systems*. New York: McGraw-Hill.

Miller, R. S., Perlman, D., & Brehm, S. S. (2007). *Intimate relationships*. New York: McGraw-Hill.

Nicholis, G., & Prigogene, I. (1989). *Exploring complexity*. New York: W.H. Freeman.

Perry, W. G. (1975). *Forms of ethical and intellectual development in the college years*. New York: Holt, Rinehart & Winston.

Piaget, J. (1972). Intellectual evolution from adolescence to adulthood. *Human Development, 15*, 1–12.

Piaget, J., & Inhelder, B. (1969). *The psychology of the child.* New York: Basic Books.

Pinker, S. (2011). *The better angels of our nature: Why violence has declined.* New York: Viking.

Pool, R. (1989). Is it healthy to be chaotic? *Science, 243*, 604–607.

Prigogene, I. (1980). *From being to becoming.* San Francisco: Freeman.

Prigogene, I., & Stengers, I. (1984). *Order out of chaos: Man's new dialogue with nature.* New York: Bantam.

Pruitt, D., & Rubin, J. (1986). *Social conflict.* New York: Random House.

Regan, P. (2011). *Close relationships.* New York: Routledge.

Riegel, K. F. (1973). Postformal operations: The final period of cognitive development. *Human Development, 16*, 346–370.

Riegel, K. F. (1975). Adult life crises: A postformal interpretation of development. In N. Datan & L. Ginsberg (Eds.), *Lifespan developmental psychology: Normative life crises* (pp. 99–129). New York: Academic Press.

Riegel, K. F. (1976). Toward a postformal theory of development. *American Psychologist, 31*, 679–700.

Riegel, K. F. (1977). Past and future trends in gerontology. *The Gerontologist, 17*, 105–113.

Rifkin, J. (2009). *The empathic civilization.* New York: Tarcher.

Robertson, H. P., & Noonan, T. W. (1968). *Relativity and cosmology.* Philadelphia: W.B. Saunders.

Rogers, D. R. B. (1989). *The effect of dyad interaction and marital adjustment on cognitive performance in everyday logical problem-solving.* Doctoral dissertation, Utah State University, Logan, UT.

Rogers, D., Sinnott, J., & van Dusen, L. (1991, July). *Marital adjustment and social cognitive performance in everyday logical problem-solving.* Paper presented at the 6th Adult Development Conference, Boston, MA.

Russell, B. (1969). *The A B C of relativity.* New York: Mentor Books.

Satir, V. (Ed.) (1967). *Conjoint family therapy.* Palo Alto, CA: Science and Behavior Books.

Scarf, M. (1987). *Intimate partners: Patterns in love and marriage.* New York: Random House.

Scarf, M. (1995). *Intimate worlds: Life inside the family.* New York: Random House.

Schlick, M. (1970). Causality in contemporary physics. In J. Toulmin, *Physical reality: Philosophical essays on 20th century physics* (pp. 83–121). New York: Harper & Row.

Schwartz, R., & Olds, J. (2000). *Marriage in motion: The ebb and flow of lasting relationships.* Cambridge, MA: Perseus Publishing.

Sheldrake, R. (1981). *A new science of life.* Los Angeles: Tarcher.

Sheldrake, R. (1989). *The presence of the past: Morphic resonance and the habits of nature.* New York: Viking.

Sheldrake, R. (1990). *The rebirth of nature.* London: Century.

Sillars, A. (1986). *Manual for coding interpersonal conflict.* Unpublished manuscript, University of Montana, Department of Interpersonal Communications.

Sinnott, J. D. (1975). Everyday thinking and Piagetian operativity in adults. *Human Development, 18,* 430–444.

Sinnott, J. D. (1977). Sex-role inconstancy, biology, and successful aging: A postformal model. *The Gerontologist, 17,* 459–463.

Sinnott, J. D. (1981). The theory of relativity: A metatheory for development? *Human Development, 24,* 293–311.

Sinnott, J. D. (1982). Correlates of sex roles in older adults. *Journal of Gerontology, 37,* 587–594.

Sinnott, J. D. (1984a). Older men, older women: Are their perceived sex roles similar? *Sex Roles, 10,* 847–856.

Sinnott, J. D. (1984b). Postformal reasoning: The relativistic stage. In M. Commons, F. Richards, & C. Armon (Eds.), *Beyond formal operations* (pp. 298–325). New York: Praeger.

Sinnott, J. D. (1985). *The expression of postformal, relativistic self-referential operations in everyday problem-solving performance.* Paper presented at the Second Beyond Formal Operations Conference at Harvard University, Cambridge, MA.

Sinnott, J. D. (1986a). *Sex roles and aging: Theory and research from a systems perspective.* New York: S. Karger.

Sinnott, J. D. (1986b). Social cognition: The construction of self-referential truth? *Educational Gerontology, 12,* 335–338.

Sinnott, J. D. (1987). Sex roles in adulthood and old age. In D. B. Carter (Ed.), *Current conceptions of sex roles and sex typing* (pp. 155–180). New York: Praeger.

Sinnott, J. D. (1989a). Changing the known, knowing the changing. In D. Kramer & M. Bopp (Eds.), *Transformation in clinical and developmental psychology* (pp. 51–69). New York: Springer.

Sinnott, J. D. (Ed.) (1989b). *Everyday problem-solving: Theory and applications.* New York: Praeger.

Sinnott, J. D. (1989c). General systems theory: A rationale for the study of everyday memory. In L. Poon, D. Rubin, & B. Wilson (Eds.), *Everyday cognition in adulthood and old age* (pp. 59–70). New Rochelle, NY: Cambridge University Press.

Sinnott, J. D. (1989d). Lifespan relativistic Postformal thought. In M. Commons, J. Sinnott, F. Richards, & C. Armon (Eds.), *Beyond formal operations I* (pp. 239–278). New York: Praeger.

Sinnott, J. D. (1990). *Yes, it's worth the trouble. Unique contributions from everyday cognition studies.* Paper presented at the Twelfth West Virginia University Conference on Lifespan Developmental Psychology: Mechanisms of Everyday Cognition, Morgantown, WV.

Sinnott, J. D. (1991a). *Conscious adult development: Complex thought and solving our intragroup conflicts.* Invited presentation, Sixth Adult Development Conference, Suffolk University, Boston.

Sinnott, J. D. (1991b). Limits to problem-solving: Emotion, intention, goal clarity, health, and other factors in postformal thought. In J. D. Sinnott & J. Cavanaugh (Eds.), *Bridging paradigms: Positive development in adulthood and cognitive aging.* New York: Praeger.

Sinnott, J. D. (1991c). What do we do to help John? A case study of everyday problem-solving in a family making decisions about an acutely psychotic member. In J. D. Sinnott & J. Cavanaugh (Eds.), *Bridging paradigms: Positive development in adulthood and cognitive aging* (pp. 203–220). New York: Praeger.

Sinnott, J. D. (1992). *Development and yearning: Cognitive aspects of spiritual development.* Paper presented at the American Psychological Association Conference, Washington, DC.

Sinnott, J. D. (1993a). Teaching in a chaotic new physics world: Teaching as a dialogue with reality. In P. Kahaney, J. Janangelo, & L. Perry (Eds.), *Theoretical and critical perspectives on teacher change* (pp. 91–108). Norwood, NJ: Ablex.

Sinnott, J. D. (1993b). Use of complex thought and resolving intragroup conflicts: A means to conscious adult development in the workplace. In J. Demick & P. M. Miller (Eds.), *Development in the workplace* (pp. 155–175). Hillsdale, NJ: Lawrence Erlbaum.

Sinnott, J. D. (1994a). Development and yearning: Cognitive aspects of spiritual development. *Journal of Adult Development, 1*, 91–99.

Sinnott, J. D. (1994b). *Interdisciplinary handbook of adult lifespan learning.* Westport, CT: Greenwood.

Sinnott, J. D. (1994c). New science models for teaching adults: Teaching as a dialogue with reality. In J. D. Sinnott (Ed.), *Interdisciplinary handbook of adult lifespan learning* (pp. 90–104). Westport, CT: Greenwood.

Sinnott, J. D. (1994d). The future of adult lifespan learning. In J. D. Sinnott (Ed.), *Interdisciplinary handbook of adult lifespan learning* (pp. 449–466). Westport, CT: Greenwood.

Sinnott, J. D. (1994e). The relationship of postformal learning and lifespan development. In J. D. Sinnott (Ed.), *Interdisciplinary handbook of adult lifespan learning* (pp. 105–119). Westport, CT: Greenwood.

Sinnott, J. D. (1996). The developmental approach: Postformal thought as adaptive intelligence. In F. Blanchard-Fields & T. Hess (Eds.), *Perspectives on cognitive change in adulthood and aging* (pp. 358–383). New York: McGraw-Hill.

Sinnott, J. D. (1997a). Brief report: Complex postformal thought in skilled research administrators. *Journal of Adult Development, 4*(1), 45–53.

Sinnott, J. D. (1997b). Developmental models of midlife and aging in women: Metaphors for transcendence and for individuality in community. In J. M. Coyle (Ed.), *Women and aging: A research guide* (pp. 149–163). Westport, CT: Greenwood.

Sinnott, J. D. (1998a). Creativity and postformal thought. In C. Adams-Price (Ed.), *Creativity and aging: Theoretical and empirical approaches.* New York: Springer.

Sinnott, J. D. (1998b). New patterns: Creating the multinational problem focused university. In R. Carneiro (Ed.), *Educacao e sociedade* (pp. 160–192). Lisbon, Portugal: Gulbenkian Foundation.

Sinnott, J. D. (1998c). *The development of logic in adulthood: Postformal thought and its applications.* New York: Plenum.

Sinnott, J. D. (Special Issues Ed.) (1999). *Reinventing the university to teach both mind and heart. Journal of Adult Development, 6*(3,4).

Sinnott, J. D. (2000). Cognitive aspects of unitative states: Spiritual self-realization, intimacy, and knowing the unknowable. In M. E. Miller & A. N. West (Eds.), *Spirituality, ethics, and relationship in adulthood: Clinical and theoretical explorations* (pp. 177–198). Madison, CT: Psychosocial Press.

Sinnott, J. D. (Special Issues Ed.) (2001, 2002a, 2002b). *Spirituality and adult development. Journal of Adult Development, 8*(4), *9*(1,2).

Sinnott, J. D. (2003a). Postformal thought and adult development: Living in balance. In J. Demick & C. Andreoletti (Eds.), *Adult development.* New York: Plenum.

Sinnott, J. D. (2003b). *Spirituality, development and healing: Lessons from several cultures.* Paper presented at Loyola College Midwinter Conference on Religion and Spirituality, Columbia, MD.

Sinnott, J. D. (2003c). Teaching as nourishment for complex thought. In N. L. Diekelmann (Ed.), *Teaching the practitioners of care: New pedagogies for the health professions* (pp. 232–271). Interpretive Studies in Healthcare and the Human Services Series. Madison, WI: University of Wisconsin Press.

Sinnott, J. D. (2004a). Learning as a humanistic dialogue with reality; new theories that help us teach the whole person: Context of learning and complex thought: Implications for modern life. In T. Hagestrom (Ed.), *Stockholm lectures: Adult development and working life* (pp. 78–108). Stockholm: University of Stockholm Press.

Sinnott, J. D. (2004b). Learning as a humanistic dialogue with reality; new theories that help us teach the whole person: Complex postformal thought and its relation to adult learning, life span development, and the new sciences. In T. Hagestrom (Ed.), *Stockholm lectures: Adult development and working life* (pp. 109–152). Stockholm: University of Stockholm Press.

Sinnott, J. D. (2004c). *Learning as a humanistic dialogue with reality; new theories that help us teach the whole person: Context of learning and complex thought: Implications for modern life.* Invited monograph, University of Stockholm, Stockholm, Sweden.

Sinnott, J. D. (2004d). *Learning as a humanistic dialogue with reality; new theories that help us teach the whole person: Complex postformal thought and its relation to adult learning, lifespan development, and the new sciences.* Invited monograph, University of Stockholm, Stockholm, Sweden.

Sinnott, J. D. (2005), The dance of the transforming self: Both feelings of connection and complex thought are needed for learning. In M. A. Wolf (Ed.), *Adulthood, new terrain, new directions* (pp. 27–38). San Francisco: Jossey Bass.

Sinnott, J. D. (2006) Spirituality as "feeling connected with the transcendent": Outline of a transpersonal psychology of adult development of self. *Religion, Spirituality, and the Scientific Study of Religion, 16*, 287–308.

Sinnott, J. D. (2007). Cognitive and representational development in adults. In K. Cartwright (Ed.), *Flexibility in literacy processes and instructional practice: Implications of developing representational ability for literacy teaching and learning.* New York: Guilford Publications.

Sinnott, J. D. (2008a). Humanistic psychology, learning, and teaching the "whole person". *I-manager's Journal on Educational Psychology, 1*(4), 55–63.

Sinnott, J. D. (2008b). Neo-Piagetian concepts of cognitive development in adults. In M. C. Smith & N. DeFratis-Densch (Eds.), *Handbook of research on adult learning and development.* Hillsdale, NJ: Lawrence Erlbaum.

Sinnott, J. D. (Special Issue Ed.) (2009a). *Complex thought and construction of identity. Journal of Adult Development, 16.*

Sinnott, J. D. (2009b). Complex thought and construction of the self in the face of aging and death. *Journal of Adult Development, 16*(3), 155–165.

Sinnott, J. D. (2009c). Introduction to the special issue: Complex thought and construction of identity. *Journal of Adult Development, 16*(3), 129–130.

Sinnott, J. D. (2009d). Introduction to the special issue: Positive psychology and adult development, Part I. *Journal of Adult Development, 17*(2), 57–58.

Sinnott, J. D. (Special Issue Ed.) (2009e). *Positive psychology and adult development, Parts I & II. Journal of Adult Development, 17.*

Sinnott, J. D. (2010a). Coherent themes: Individuals' relationships with God, and their early childhood experiences, bonds with significant others, and relational delusions during psychotic episodes have common existential and relational themes. *Journal of Adult Development, 17*(4), 230–244.

Sinnott, J. D. (2010b). Introduction to the special issue: Positive psychology and adult development, Part II. *Journal of Adult Development, 17,* 191–192.

Sinnott, J. D. (Special Issue Ed.) (2010c). *Positive psychology and adult development: Part I.* Special edition. *Journal of Adult Development.*

Sinnott, J. D. (2011) Constructing the self in the face of aging and death: Complex thought and learning. In C. Hoare (Ed.), *Oxford handbook of adult development and learning,* 2nd ed. (pp. 248–264). New York: Oxford University Press.

Sinnott, J. D. (Ed.) (2013). *Positive psychology: Advances in understanding adult motivation.* New York: Springer.

Sinnott, J. D., & Berlanstein, D. (2006). The importance of feeling whole: Learning to "feel connected," community and adult development. In C. H. Hoare (Ed.), *Oxford handbook of adult development and learning* (pp. 381–406). New York: Oxford University Press.

Sinnott, J. D., Block, M., Grambs, J., Gaddy, C., & Davidson, J. (1980). *Sex roles in mature adults: Antecedents and correlates.* College Park, MD: Center on Aging, University of Maryland College Park.

Sinnott, J. D., & Cavanaugh, J. (Eds.) (1991). *Bridging paradigms: Positive development in adulthood and cognitive aging.* New York: Praeger.

Sinnott, J. D., Geissler, T., Hilton, S., Merson, J., Nardini, A., Newman, R., Probst, A., Schluter, R., & Tippett, C. (2013). *Cognition and relationship quality.* Paper presented at the 25th Annual Convention of the Association for Psychological Science, Washington, DC.

Sinnott J. D., & Guttmann, D. (1978a). Piagetian logical abilities and older adults' abilities to solve everyday problems. *Human Development, 21,* 327–333.

Sinnott, J. D., & Guttmann, D. (1978b). The dialectics of decision making in older adults. *Human Development, 21,* 190–200.

Sinnott, J. D., & Johnson, L. (1996). *Reinventing the university: A radical proposal for a problem focused university.* Norwood, NJ: Ablex.

Sinnott, J. D., & Rabin, J. S. (2010). Sex roles revisited. In V. S. Ramachandran (Ed.), *Encyclopedia of Human Behavior* (Vol. 323, pp. 1–7). New York: Elsevier.

Sinnott, R., & Spencer, F. (1996). Reconsidering sex roles and aging: Preliminary data on some influences of context, cohort, time. ERIC. Document #ED 391 139/CG 026 796.

Sinnott, J. D., & Shifren, K. (2002). Gender and aging: Transforming and transcending gender roles. In J. Birren & K. W. Schaie (Eds.), *Handbook of the psychology of aging,* 5th ed. San Diego: Academic Press.

Smith, H. (1991). *The world's religions.* San Francisco: Harper.

Smith, H. (1994). *The illustrated world's religions.* San Francisco: Harper.

Smith, H. (2001). *Why religion matters: The fate of the human spirit in an age of disbelief.* New York: HarperCollins.

Smith, H. (2012). *The Huston Smith reader.* Berkeley, CA: University of California Press.

Smith, L. B., & Thelan, E. (Eds.) (1993). *A dynamic systems approach to development.* Cambridge, MA: MIT Press.

Spanier, G. B. (1976). Measuring dyadic adjustment: New scales for assessing the quality of marriage and similar dyads. *Journal of Marriage and the Family, 38,* 15–28.

Spanier, G. B. (1989). *DAS users' manual.* New York: Multi-Health Systems.

Stafford, L., & Canary, D. J. (1991). Maintenance strategies and romantic relationship type, gender, and relational characteristics. *Journal of Social and Personal Relationships, 8,* 217–242.

Stafford, L., Dainton, M., & Hass, S. (2000). Measuring routine and strategic relational maintenance: Scale development, sex vs gender roles, and the prediction of relational characteristics. *Communication Monographs, 67,* 306–323.

Stanovich, K. E., West, R. F., & Toplak, M. E. (2013). Myside bias, rational thinking, and intelligence. *Current Directions in Psychological Science, 22,* 259–264.

Sternberg. R. J. (1998). *Cupid's arrow.* Cambridge, UK: Cambridge University Press.

Sternberg, R. J. (1986). A triangular theory of love. *Psychological Review, 93,* 119–135.

Toulmin, J. (1970). *Physical reality: Philosophical essays on 20th century physics.* New York: Harper & Row.

Vallacher, R. R., Coleman, P. T., Nowack, A., & Bui-Wrzosinska, L. (2010). Rethinking intractable conflict. *American Psychologist, 65*, 262–278.

von Bertalanfy, L. (1968). *General systems theory.* New York: Braziller.

von Neumann, J., & Morgenstern, O. (1947). *Theory of games and economic behavior.* Princeton, NJ: Princeton University Press.

Waldrop, M. (1992). *Complexity: The emerging science at the edge of order and chaos.* New York: Simon and Schuster.

Weiner, N. (1961). *Cybernetics.* Cambridge, MA: MIT Press.

Welwood, J. (1996). *Love and awakening.* New York: HarperCollins.

Westen, D. (2007). *The political brain.* Cambridge, MA: The Perseus Group.

Windle, M., & Sinnott, J. D. (1985). A psychometric study of the Bem Sex Role Inventory with an older adult sample. *Journal of Gerontology, 40*, 336–343.

Wolf, F. A. (1981). *Taking the quantum leap.* New York: Harper & Row.

Wood, M., Hilton, S., Spanos, E., & Sinnott, J. D. (submitted for publication). *Flow, mindfulness, cognitive flexibility, and postformal thought* [paper available from the 4th author].

Yan, B. (1995). *Nonabsolute/relativistic (N/R) thinking: A possible unifying commonality underlying models of postformal reasoning.* Ph.D. dissertation, University of British Columbia, Vancouver.

Yan, B., & Arlin, P. K. (1995). Non-absolute/relativistic thinking: A common factor underlying models of postformal reasoning? *Journal of Adult Development, 2*, 223–240.

Zukav, G. (1979). *The dancing Wu Li masters: An overview of the new physics.* New York: Bantam.

About the Author

Jan D. Sinnott, Ph.D., is Professor of Psychology at Towson University in Baltimore, MD, and a licensed psychologist. She specializes in lifespan positive development and the applications of existential, transpersonal, mind–body, and positive psychology. After completing a postdoc at the National Institute on Aging, she developed her theory of complex problem-solving in adulthood, termed complex postformal thought. She has authored or co-authored over 100 scholarly and applied books and publications. Her research team is currently studying complex problem-solving, intelligence, mindfulness, concepts of the self, and satisfaction in intimate relationships.

Index

Note: Page numbers followed by the letter "f" indicate material found in figures.